Composers' Houses

D1418855

Composers' Houses

Gérard Gefen

Photography
Christine Bastin
Jacques Evrard

SEVEN DIALS

Contents

PAGE 1: *Ole Bull's house at Lysøen, in Norway.*

PAGE 2: *Puccini's piano at Torre del Lago.*

PAGE 4: *Chopin's writing desk at the Château de Nohant, the home of George Sand.*

Composers and Their Houses

Writers are free people. They can work almost anywhere, in an apartment at the heart of the city, in a cabin secluded deep in the woods, in a hotel room on a tropical island, on a boat, in China, or yet in prison. The simplest materials will suffice for their purposes—a scrap of paper, a wax tablet, a pen, a stick of charcoal. Indeed, some writers are happy merely to dictate. Scribblers can remain aloof from that hypocritical fellow creature, the reader, and even leave to the mails whatever relationship they have with their foster father, the editor.

Musicians enjoy no such freedom. Whether composing at a desk or on a piano, they nearly always remain dependent upon the latter to improvise a melody or to verify the sound of a chord. They must also make themselves available to interpreters, patrons, friends, and pupils, all of whom figure among their means of livelihood. Musicians, almost invariably, come in contact with the theatre, where they may find themselves torn between the turbulent world of impresarios, performers, and critics and a desire for quietude, the peace of mind so essential to the mental work of composition. Such contradictory allures are reflected even in the holiday houses illustrated in this book, where several of the summer residences are in the solitude of mountains or forests, whereas others are in fashionable watering places frequented by the smart set making their social rounds as the "seasons" dictate.

Finally, it is worth noting that, far more than most writers, composers are family men. This should not surprise, given that very often it is within the family that musicians discover their art. Sometimes it even comes to them as a legacy bestowed by a veritable dynasty.

Composers, furthermore, are constantly on the go, touring as virtuosos or conductors, attending or taking part in the premieres of their works. On the way home, they find themselves laden with laurel crowns—sometimes fashioned of painted iron—garnered in Saint Petersburg or Milan, decorations representing various exotic orders, full-length portraits of divas, their own busts cast in bronze, a thousand mementoes proffered by young or even mature admirers. In other words, traveling light is out of the question. And prophets being seldom acknowledged in their own countries, composers may very well find it expedient to pack up everything—house, home, piano, and souvenirs—and relocate abroad.

All such factors give the composer's house a character frequently quite different from that of a writer. Like painters or sculptors, composers place the vital center of existence in the studio, a music room filled with such indispensable accessories as pianos, violins, and other instruments, music stands, metronomes, and huge sheets of scored paper.

Of course, there is no typical composer's house any more than there is a typical composer. From Haydn to Poulenc, the language, the style, and the genres of music have altered, and so too the ways in which musicians practice their craft—much more, in fact, than the language, style, and genres of literature or the writer's profession. Of course, urban life, the feeling for nature, and modes of travel have also undergone radical change in the course of two centuries. Of course, we shall see childhood homes and retirement houses, and find ourselves breathless imagining the frenzied itinerary that led from the former to the latter. Of course, personalities differ, as witnessed by Johannes Brahms and Johann Strauss the Younger, who frequented the same places but had little else in common, or by the flamboyant Ole Bull and the discreet Edvard Grieg, both of them Norwegian, or by Franz Liszt and his son-in-law, the tumultuous Richard Wagner, or yet by those contemporaries and friends, Maurice Ravel and Manuel de Falla. However, save for a few quite particular cases—Beethoven walled up inside his deafness or Schubert with his unmentionable disease—the masters lived in houses that still resonate those mute and mysterious harmonies, the famous silence which, after the last chord has been sounded, remains that of a long-departed genius.

And what a pity that the dislocations of history make it impossible for us pay a call on Vivaldi (Campo Sacharia, behind the Pietà), or Johann Sebastian Bach (how ever did he managed to house all those children?), or Mendelssohn (would he show us his beautiful sketchbooks?), or César Franck (I actually lived, somewhat frustrated, in the apartment house next door), or yet Stravinsky, at the time of his residence at Clarens near Lac Léman, in the street subsequently renamed Rue du Sacre-du-Printemps.

But would this afford us greater insight into *The Creation,* the *"Skittles Trio," Les Troyens,* or the *Symphony on a French Mountain Air?* Marcel Proust, in *Contre Sainte-Beuve,* warned us that when it comes to a major talent certain questions are simply irrelevant, questions such as: "How was he affected by the spectacle of nature? What was his attitude towards women or money? Was he rich or poor; what was his regimen, his quotidian way of life?"

In this, Proust was surely right, for a work of art is sufficient unto itself. Still, who could fail to be touched by the tiny barn in Vinci where Leonardo was born, the Possonière manor house emblazoned with the arms of Ronsard, or the Vallée aux Loups cherished by Chateaubriand—all places in which one can sense a fraternal bond with gifted human beings merely by treading the same ground.

One must also retain a sense of proportion, as well as a modicum of humor. Visiting the Verdi villa outside Parma does not constitute an act of ecstatic adoration, of a sort at least still manifest at the tomb of Rudolph Valentino. Nor does it satisfy the need, for example, to discover some relationship between the pattern in the tapistery on the wall and the harmonic scheme of *Falstaff!* Yet, it is fun to note that in the park the composer could not resist the temptation to dub an artificial cave, built for cold storage, "the tomb of Aïda."

Moreover, the residences of great creators, by virtue of their having been better preserved than the dwellings of their anonymous contemporaries, bear a different order of witness. The furnishings, decorations, and bibelots exhibited there reflect the life-style and taste of their respective periods. Frequently, composers' houses, being more worldly places as well as, admittedly, more conformist places, are richer in their historical revelations than the habitations of writers or plastic artists.

Finally, a house is also a work of art, in the more material sense of the term. Several of the musicians revisited here understood this so well that they became their own architects. Proust knew it too, as he revealed, again, in his attack on the Sainte-Beuve style of biographical critique, declaring that "each hour of our life, even as it dies, reincarnates itself and hides in some concrete object."

— *G é r a r d   G e f e n*

Joseph

Haydn

1732–1809

Throughout his long career, Joseph Haydn merely made do with whatever housing came with his current post, and little is known about those arrangements, even though their beneficiary was the most celebrated musician of his generation.

Stendahl, moved by eye-witness accounts, deftly summarized Haydn's everyday existence in a few short sentences: "His life was well regulated and rich in tranquillity. Rising early in the morning, he dressed in proper attire, took his place at a small table next to the piano, and generally returned there after his midday dinner. In the evening he attended rehearsals or the opera, the latter given four times a week at the princely palace. Sometimes, though infrequently, he spent the first part of the day hunting. . . ."

Haydn, true to his time, always sought the security of regular employment, unlike the greatest composers of the next generation—pre-Romantics such as Mozart and Beethoven—who would opt for independence. Haydn was born on 31 March or 1 April 1732 at Rohrau in Lower Austria, where his father, an amateur musician as well as a wheelwright, enjoyed the status of a minor notable. Early recognized as musically gifted, Joseph was sent at the age of nine to the choir school at St. Stephen's Cathedral in Vienna. Scarcely had the boy soprano arrived when, on 28 July 1741, he sang in the Requiem Mass for Antonio Vivaldi, who had just died in the Austrian capital. As soon as his voice broke Haydn had to leave the choir, an event that quickly ushered him into a period of considerable difficulty lasting several years. For a time Haydn was the pupil of the singer and composer Nicola Porpora, to whom he also provided keyboard accompaniment and occasionally even valet service. Finally, in 1759, he received his first stable employment, as director of music to Count

Morzin. By then Haydn had already compiled an impressive catalogue of original works: some 20 of his 104 symphonies, 10 quartets, the latter a new and very popular genre, and numerous sonatas. His living secured, Haydn took a wife, marrying the sister of the young woman he actually loved, as Mozart would do a generation later. The union proved unhappy and ultimately childless.

In 1760 Count Morzin, for reasons of economy, found himself obliged to disband his orchestra. Fortunately, Prince Paul Anton Esterházy had come to know the orchestra as well as to appreciate one of young Haydn's works, very likely the composition today identified as Symphony No. 1. By 1 May 1761 Haydn could breathe easily, having been engaged by the Prince as *Vice-Kapellmeister,* the *Ober-Kapellmeister* ("Principal Court Musician") being the elderly Gregor Joseph Werner. For almost forty years thereafter he would remain in service to the House of Esterházy, one of the most powerful families within the Austrian Empire. Although Hungarian, the Esterházys spent most of their time either at Palais Esterházy in Vienna's Wallnerstrasse or at the baroque Schloss Eisenstadt, some fifty kilometers from the capital.

In March 1762 Prince Paul Anton died and was succeeded by his younger brother Nikolaus. A great lover of both music and theatre, Prince Nikolaus lost no time reckoning with the pleasure and prestige to be garnered from the genius of his younger Kapellmeister. In his own right the new Prince could boast evolved talents for both the violin and the baryton. The latter, a cousin of the viola d'amore, had a second range of

*"I*ts quietude and tranquillity pleased me," said Haydn of the house in which he would spend his retirement in Gumpendorf, a suburb

on the southwest side of Vienna. ABOVE: *Portrait of Haydn, miniature on ivory painted by an unknown artist.*

The Pensioner of Gumpendorf

strings behind the neck, which, though primarily intended for resonance, provided a special effect when plucked with the thumb. Haydn soon found his salary increased, and in 1776, following the death of the Ober-Kapellemeister, he assumed the full dignity of that post. Now he acquired a pretty little house in Eisenstadt at Klostergasse 82, close by the castle. The price—2,000 florins—represented several years of salary, and to meet it the musician had to borrow about one-third from his brother-in-law.

In the end Haydn found only slight pleasure in his house on Klostergasse. Twice it would burn down, the first time in August 1768. Prince Nikolaus had the dwelling rebuilt at his own expense, but Haydn, weary of the whole thing and ever cautious, sold the property in 1778, several weeks after the second fire. In 1766, moreover, Prince Nikolaus launched into the construction of a new castle, Esterháza, on the site of a hunting lodge at Süttör—today Fertöd—approximately fifty kilometers south of Eisenstadt. It was at this grandiose *Schloss*, soon known as the "Hungarian Versailles," that Haydn would henceforth live for most of the year. Otherwise, he followed the Prince whenever the latter traveled to Vienna or to one of his other castles.

only to compose (most notably some twenty operas) but also to rehearse the orchestra and soloists, conduct galas, operas, concerts, and religious services, and generally manage what was a vast enterprise of private spectacle.

Meanwhile, the fame of Joseph Haydn spread, to such a degree that his works were both published and played virtually everywhere in Europe. The composer, nonetheless, remained tied to Prince Nikolaus, whose service he had promised never to leave. But on 18 September 1790 the Prince died, whereupon his successor, Prince Anton, temporarily dismissed his Kapelle. Several weeks later the fifty-eight-year-old Haydn set out upon his first long journey, which took him all the way to Georgian London for what became a triumphant season (1791–1792). Then, following a brief interlude in Vienna, he departed anew, no less covered in glory,

At the bottom of the magnificent gardens at Esterháza, Nikolaus had built the "Musikhaus," a pavilion for his musicians and other employees. Only Haydn and the court doctor enjoyed as many as four rooms each. Staff musicians, who would soon be required to leave their families behind, had to live two to a room. These conditions, as well as the frequently extended sojourns at Esterháza, gave rise to the famous *Farewell Symphony* (No. 45), in which the players drop out one after the other—a hint to the Prince that he should permit his musicians to rejoin their families at Eisenstadt. Haydn, a true workaholic, undertook not

OPPOSITE AND ABOVE: *The lawned inner courtyard and the present door opening to the recreated interior of Haydn's Gumpendorf house. With its* *simplicity and calm, the dwelling stood in marked contrast to the turbulent life led by the composer during his long years at Esterháza and Eisenstadt.*

for the second of his two seasons in England (1794–1795). In between them, his wife had discovered a house she wanted to buy at Kleine Steingasse 73 (today Haydngasse) in Gumpendorf, then a suburb of the Austrian capital, on the road to Schönbrunn. "The quietude and tranquillity pleased me," Haydn wrote, "[and so] I bought the property and had an upper story built during my second sojourn in London." Even after he had re-entered Prince Anton's service, which took him back to Eisenstadt and Esterháza from time to time, Haydn would live in his own house, beginning in the spring of 1797. Finally, at the age of sixty-five, the great man was at home, under his own roof, for the first time.

The simple, pleasant exterior, with its grassy courtyard, remains largely unaltered, but little is known about the interior furnishings during Haydn's years in Gumpendorf. Camille Pleyel, son of the French piano manufacturer, who visited the house in 1805, noted: "The house is very pretty and very well fitted out. . . ." Young Pleyel, however, was only sixteen at the time and had little experience in household matters. Still, one may assume that the arrangements were modest as well as tasteful and perhaps a bit conventional. Albert Christoph Dies, for example, has left an account of the thirty visits he paid to Haydn between 1805 and 1808. Dies, being a painter, would surely have noted any striking details, had they existed. Another witness, this one from 1808, tells us that "next to one room was an alcove ornamented with small sheets of music composed [by Haydn], written in his own hand, and framed with flowers." It is also known that the musician owned a good number of engravings and a gray, red-tailed parrot that greeted visitors by squawking "Papa Haydn!" He also boasted two pianos, one a large Érard and the other a Longman and Broderip. Finally, we know that his library contained a hundred books, eight of them banned by the censor.

The term "pensioner" introduced at the head of this chapter is scarcely adequate as a characterization of Haydn at Gumpendorf. If the composer was now largely free of demands, by comparison with his former life at Esterháza, he nonetheless continued to write music, and it is from this period that we have several of his greatest masterpieces, among them *The Seven Last Words* (1796), *The Creation* (1798), *The Seasons* (1801), and a few of his most beautiful Masses. Haydn never truly stopped working until illness overtook him in 1803.

Haydn's last days were troubled by war. In 1805, following the Battle of Ulm, Napoleon entered Vienna. On 10 May 1809 the Grand Army returned to the Austrian capital, bombarding it mercilessly. Cannon roared all around Gumpendorf, sending a bomb fragment into the composer's own courtyard. On 12 May, Vienna surrendered. Napoleon, learning that Joseph Haydn lived on the outskirts, had an honor guard posted at the Kleine Steingasse, to make certain its most famous resident would be left in peace. Haydn died a few days later, on 31 May 1809.

The funeral service took place on 15 June at Vienna's Schottenkirche, which was thronged with almost as many French officers as there were the notable of Vienna.

OPPOSITE AND ABOVE: *The interior of Haydn's Gumpendorf house as presently reconstituted and filled with contemporary furniture designed by Elsa Prochazka. "From my earliest childhood, my parents made every effort to endow me with habits of cleanliness and order. These two things became second nature to me," Haydn told a visitor to Gumpendorf.*

Wolfgang Amadeus
Mozart

1756–1791

Wolfgang Amadeus Mozart, during his child-prodigy tours in Germany, Italy, England, and France, rarely stayed put for very long, but at home in Salzburg, he relocated only once in the first twenty-eight years of his life there. In 1773 Leopold Mozart removed his brood from the house at Getreidegasse 9, where Wolfgang had come into the world on 27 January 1756, two floors above an upscale grocery shop owned by the landlord. The family then settled into a larger flat at Markatplatz 8 on the opposite bank of the River Salzach. Here Wolfgang lived following his return to Salzburg in 1783, and here as well Leopold would die in 1787.

During the second part of his life, however—a period which included that "Golden Age" decade in Vienna—Mozart would experience a far less stable existence. Indeed, by the time of his tragically premature death in 1791, the composer had lived in no less than thirteen different houses. Yet, Mozart never knew the kind of domestic upheaval characteristic of so many creative individuals, among them the agitated Ludwig van Beethoven. Rather, it was material necessity or some turn in his private or professional life that drove Mozart on every occasion when he packed up and moved on.

"Finally, my blood boiled over and I said: 'So, Your Grace is no longer satisfied with me?' 'What's this, the cretin thinks he can threaten me! There's the door, over there; I want nothing further to do with such a miserable subject.' I then retorted: 'I feel the same and want nothing more to do with you!' 'Well, be off!' And so, withdrawing, I shot back: 'Fine, let's call it quits! Tomorrow you shall have my resignation!'"

Thus ended, according to Mozart, his stormy relationship with his patron, Count Hieronymus Colloredo, the Prince/Archbishop of Salzburg. The scene occurred in Vienna on 2 May 1781. That same evening, Mozart left the house on Singerstrasse, where he had lodged together other members of the Colloredo suite, and began boarding with Frau Weber on the Graben.

Maria-Caecilia Weber was none other than the mother of Aloysia, the young lady with whom Mozart had become infatuated three years earlier in Mannheim. Now installed in Vienna, Frau Weber let rooms in her large flat in the house known as "God's Eye" (*Zum Augen Gottes*), Am Peter 11. Leopold Mozart, always

*T*he flat in the house ("Figaro-Haus") at Schülerstrasse 846 was the most sumptuous that Mozart ever occupied in Vienna, as witnessed by the staircase and its decorated ceiling.

ABOVE: *The portrait of Mozart painted by his brother-in-law, Joseph Lange.*

A Musician with Thirteen Addresses

ABOVE: *It was here that Mozart composed* The Marriage of Figaro, *the* Prague Symphony, *and eight of his most beautiful piano concertos.*

opposed to his son's involvement with the Weber family, wasted no time protesting the move. The criticism finally had its effect, when, four months later, Mozart repacked his bags and moved all of two steps away. And this despite the unavailability of Aloysia, who shortly before had married the painter Joseph Lange, the author of a rare authentic portrait of the composer. Not to be outdone, Mozart merely transferred his attentions to her younger sister, Constanze, whom he would marry on 4 August 1782.

The young couple set up in a small flat in a house known as "The Red Sabre." By the end of the year, with Constanze pregnant and the apartment far too small, they went to live with one of Mozart's admirers, Baron Wezlar von Plankenstern. After three months, however, Baron Wezlar was obliged to reclaim the rooms, on which he had never charged rent. Now the patron even volunteered to underwrite the temporary lodgings to which the Mozarts moved. Here they would remain only a few weeks before relocating again, this time into a flat on the Judenplatz.

On 31 July 1783 Mozart and Constanze traveled to Salzburg for a visit with Leopold, returning to Vienna only at the end of November. In the meantime, their first child, born on 17 June, had died while in the care of a wet nurse. Fleeing sad memories, the distraught parents did not go back to the Judenplatz but, instead, accepted the hospitality of another admirer, Maria Theresia von Trattner, a pianist and the wife of one of Vienna's foremost publishers. In a large room at the Trattnerhof block of flats, Wolfgang gave a series of very successful "academies," private concerts organized for the Viennese uppercrust. The child prodigy having now grown up, the onetime employee of Archbishop Colloredo hoped that his audacity and independent spirit would be rewarded.

The Mozarts nonetheless left the Trattnerhof at the end of September, a sudden development for which several motives have been proposed. One involves a growing warmth of feeling between Wolfgang and Maria Theresia, which finally alarmed both her husband and his wife. There was also the birth, on 21 September 1784, of Karl-Thomas, the elder of the Mozarts' two children who survived, cause enough for the couple to seek a place of their own. Too, the composer's financial situation had vastly improved. In fact, the rent on their new apartment, at Schülerstrasse 846, was 460 florins, a sum equal to the annual salary Wolfgang had received in Salzburg. Mozart himself described the new residence as "a beautiful home, handsomely fitted out." Here he would remain for the next two and half years, a period that must have been one of the happiest for the musician, because it was in the Schülerstrasse that he composed many of his greatest masterpieces. Among these was *The Marriage of Figaro,* which accounts for the present name of the dwelling: "Figaro-Haus."

In 1787, however, Mozart had to face up to the reality that he was living far beyond his means. In the spring he took a less expensive apartment in the Landstrasse, near the home of his friend Gottfried von Jacquin, to whose family he had dedicated the *"Skittles Trio"* (*Kegelstatt,* Clarinet Trio in E flat) in memory of the games played in their garden. Still, having once more failed to pay his rent, Mozart migrated a few months later to a small street giving on to the Graben.

On 7 December 1787 Emperor Joseph II had named Mozart "composer to the Imperial and royal household," a sonorous title offering heavy duties and only light income. With the relative failure of *Don Giovanni* in Vienna, Mozart was yet again compelled by pecuniary woes to change addresses. In June 1788 he moved his family into a suburban house known as the "Three Fires" *(Zum den drei Feuern)*, a name that no doubt amused the Freemason composer.

Thanks to a successful revival of *Figaro*, Mozart's finances improved considerably during the late months of 1789. On the feast of Saint Sylvester, the musician, together with his friend Joseph Haydn, staged a house warming at his new residence in the Judenplatz. The Mozarts remained there until 23 September 1790, when Wolfgang left for a two-month tour of Germany. Back home in November, the family settled at 970 Rauhensteingasse, occupying a roomy apartment in the "Little Imperial Palace" *(Das Kleine Kaiserhaus)*.

This thirteenth and final residence is also the one we know the best, thanks to the inventory taken after Mozart's death. The building has since been demolished and twice reconstructed, but eye-witness accounts agree on all essential points concerning the disposition of the premises. The flat comprised some 150 square meters on the first floor up of what was a handsome building, as we know from a contemporary engraving. In addition to the large kitchen, which also functioned as a vestibule where the family's two servants slept, the suite consisted of four main rooms: a parlor, a small parlor, a bedroom which doubled as a billiard room—both Wolfgang and Costanze loved the game—and, finally, the composer's workroom.

Mozart owned a large collection of fine furniture, its many chairs (eighteen) and tables reflecting his love of society. The workroom contained a roll-top desk, a lacquered secretary, two bookcases, a "pianoforte with pedals," a viola, around sixty pieces of porcelain, glasses, a teapot, and even a pair of coffee mills. In other words, the setting in which Mozart spent his last days scarcely accords with the wretchedness conjured up by the nineteenth-century Romantics. Indeed, the composer's income had risen substantially, so that in 1791, the year he died, it reached 6,000 florins, or at least 80,000 dollars, or 132,000 pounds

sterling, in today's money. The financial problems were nonetheless real, but they derived mostly from the need to satisfy debts contracted in the past, as well as from a life-style the composer could not easily forego. Equally important was the bill from the tailor, but the worst of all came from the decorator, whose statement amounted to 80 florins (about 3,000 dollars or 5,000 pounds sterling).

It was in his studio in the corner room overlooking the street that Mozart died on Monday the 5th of December 1791 at 12:55 in the morning.

ABOVE: *T*he façade of the house where Mozart was born in Salzburg, Austria. The composer had little taste for the city, which has now turned Mozartiana into a major industry.

Ludwig van

Beethoven

1770–1827

Any attempt to place Beethoven within a settled domestic environment must deal with a number of quite special, if not unique, problems. Which dwelling, for example, should one begin with? The house in Bonn, at Bonngasse 515, where Beethoven was born on 16 or 17 December 1770, is today a museum, but it reveals little about the daily life of a young genius. Nor does it provide much insight into how the autodidact son of a mediocre, alcoholic musician could have grown up to be one of the greatest composers in the history of music. It is, rather, in Vienna, where Beethoven moved in 1793 and remained for the rest of life, that we must look for some sense of how he lived.

But where in Vienna? During his thirty-five years in the Imperial capital, Beethoven changed his address more than thirty-five times, or more than forty-five times if one counts summers in the country near Vienna or in such watering places as Baden and Mödling. While Mozart's frequent dislocations were motivated by evident necessity, nothing of the sort could be said in the case of Beethoven. At times, the younger composer, for no apparent reason, maintained several domiciles at once, much to the dismay of his contemporaries.

Even when Beethoven settled for a while, the arrangement never lasted more than three years. The first of these relatively stable periods came in November 1793, just after his arrival in Vienna when the twenty-one-year-old musician lodged in the palace of Prince Rasumowsky, remaining there until sometime in 1796. On two different occasions, first in 1804–1806 and then in 1809–1810, he occupied two rooms on the fourth floor in a house, at Mölkerbastei 8, owned by the noble Pasqualati family. Here he had a splendid view from the city's ancient ramparts towards the slopes of the Vienna Woods and the meadows of the Danube. While at this address he composed the Fourth and Fifth Symphonies as well as the Violin Concerto. Finally, from 15 October 1825 until his death on 26 March 1827 Beethoven lived in a small flat at Schwarzpanierstrasse 15.

Several other stops along Beethoven's progress through Vienna are also worth noting. One is the almost rural cottage in Heiligenstadt, for it was here, in the summer of 1802, that he drafted his famous "Testament." Although desperate and even suicidal over his growing deafness, Beethoven finally decided to go on living and, for that reason, to abandon the glittering world of his early years in Vienna: "I must live in exile. Whenever I venture into society, I am immediately seized by the most awful anxiety, the anxiety of having my condition remarked upon." During the last weeks of

ABOVE: *A caricature of Beethoven by Joseph Daniel Böhm (c. 1822). "I love a tree more than a human being," declared Beethoven. Deafness* *increasingly isolated the great composer from Viennese society, where, in any event, he had never bothered to cut a fine figure.*

1802 Beethoven was invited by Emanuel Schikaneder—theatre manager and playwright, as well librettist of *The Magic Flute*—to take up residence in the outbuildings of the Theater an der Wien, where Mozart's masterpiece had received its premiere a dozen years before. The idea was for Beethoven to compose an opera, an enterprise he would abandon, but only temporarily.

A bit later in the same year Beethoven commenced writing his Third Symphony, the *Eroica*, while ensconced at Döblinger Hauptstrasse 92, where the dwelling would thereafter be known as "Eroica-Haus." At the end of 1803 he returned to the Theater an der Wien, now to work in earnest on his *Leonora*, the first version of *Fidelio*. Thanks to Ignaz von Seyfried, Kapellmeister at the same theatre, we have an account of Beethoven's living arrangements at the time: "A truly astonishing disorder reigned throughout the household. Books and music scattered on every side, here the remains of a cold meal, over there uncorked and half-empty bottles, elsewhere a music stand with quick sketches for a new quartet, in another place the leavings from lunch; there, on the piano, scribbled sheets of music, the materials for a grandiose symphony, still in an embryonic stage; here proofs waiting to be delivered, notes from friends and business letters strewn on the floor; between the windows a decent gorgonzola, *ad latus* the substantial vestiges of a genuine Verona sausage. . . ."

Bettine Brentano and Beethoven met during the summer of 1810, which marked the beginning of

ABOVE AND OPPOSITE: *The charming inner courtyard and street door at Heiligenstadt. It was to Heiligenstadt, which still retains the rustic look of a wine-country village, that the thirty-two-year-old Beethoven retired to write his famous "Testament."*

their warm, if not amorous, relationship. Although known to the composer as "darling, darling Bettine," Frau von Arnim, as Bettine soon became, proved no more generous in her assessment of the master's domestic scene than the ironic and very possibly malicious Seyfried. In her letters to Goethe, to whom she was close, Bettine noted: "He has three refuges where he takes turn hiding: one in the country, one in the city, and another on the ramparts." She then went on to describe the apartment in the "Pasqualati-Haus": "His residence is quite remarkable: in the first room, two or three pianos, all set on the floor without legs; chests full of his affairs, a three-legged chair; in the second room, his bed which, winter and summer alike, consists of a pallet with a thin blanket, a wash basin on a pine table, nightclothes on the floor."

Nothing very different is suggested by the modest accommodations in the Schwarzpanierstrasse, where Beethoven died. The drawing made by Johann Nepomuk Hœchle reflects the same chaos. Be that as it may, the descriptions do not create the image of an obscure composer confined by neglect to miserable lodgings. The frivolous Viennese may have often preferred Rossini and his "trumperies," as Beethoven called them, to the intense, profound quartets of the German master, but many other contemporaries, throughout Europe as well as in Austria, held Beethoven to be the greatest of his century. At the premiere of the Ninth Symphony, on 7 May 1824, the audience responded so enthusiastically that it overrode official etiquette to recall the composer three times, a kind of reception normally reserved for the Imperial family.

Nor did Beethoven require expressions of pity concerning the economics of his life. While a good part of the income he enjoyed went to pay for the indiscretions of his nephew Karl, the prudent master had stashed away in a drawer certain "bank shares" amounting to a decent bit of capital. In truth, once Beethoven acknowledged the seriousness of his hearing loss, he renounced the smart world and adopted a bohemian life-style, utterly indifferent to convention or appearance.

Yet, Beethoven was essentially a merry soul, often charming, with an appetite for good food and fine wine, which he readily shared with his numerous friends. For such convivial meals, he preferred the pleasant inns of Vienna and its environs to his own cramped and disordered chambers.

OPPOSITE: *The gallery along the upper floor at Heiligenstadt.* ABOVE: *The façade of "Pasqualati-Haus," where Beethoven lived on two different occasions, and where, most notably, he composed the Fourth and Fifth Symphonies, the Fourth Piano Concerto, the Violin Concerto, and the music for Goethe's* Egmont.

Franz
Schubert
1797–1828

The history of Schubert's domestic arrangements, although quite different from those of Beethoven, are nonetheless singular in the extreme. In the whole of his life, Franz Schubert never lived alone for more than two years, and this on three occasions only, during which he occupied a tiny room in an inn.

The son of a teacher, Franz Schubert was born on 31 January 1797 in a small flat above his father's private school, at Nussdorferstrasse 54 in the Himmelpfortgrund suburb of Vienna. The "Red Crayfish House" (*Zum roten Krebsen*), as the dwelling was called, is today a museum, even though Franz did not live there much beyond his fifth year. In May 1801 Schubert Senior moved the school a short distance away, to Saülengasse 3, installing his family and his class in the "Black Horse" (*Zum schwarzen Rössel*). The Schuberts would remain at this address until 1817.

Meanwhile, Franz was sent to boarding school at the Imperial and Royal City College—the *Stadtkonvikt* ("City Seminary") near St. Stephen's Cathedral—where he performed in the choir as a scholarship pupil. Such were his musical gifts that he was allowed to stay a year beyond his change of voice, that is, until 23 November 1813. Following a stage at the Normal School, also close by St. Stephen's, Franz returned home to join his father as a teaching assistant. A friend described the scene as modest at best: "At the time of my visit during a very hard winter, I found him in a small room that was dark, damp, and without heat. He sat wrapped in an old threadbare dressing gown; he was freezing . . . and composing." Yet, contrary to romantic legend, Schubert owned a piano, actually a Konrad Graf, one of the finest to be had in contemporary Vienna.

In sheer precocity, the young composer was the equal of Mozart. By the age of twenty he had already written some 600 works, a good many of them masterpieces, such as *Gretchen am Spinnrade*, *Erlkönig*, and *Auf dem Wasser zu singen*. For the texts of his songs,

Schubert often found a fruitful source in Goethe, even though the poet himself had little feeling for music. Schubert sent him a copy of *Erlkönig* but never received so much as an acknowledgment.

In 1815 Schubert met Franz von Schober (1796–1882), a young poet of his own age from the comfortable middle classes. He lived with the Schober family on four different occasions, from December 1816 to September 1817, from 1882 through the summer of 1823, during much of 1826, and finally from March 1827 to August 1828. The environment in which Schober hospitality placed the composer can be readily imagined, given that, since 1815, the Biedermeier style had become virtually canonic for Viennese society.

The term "Biedermeier" derived from an eponymous poet invented by the German humorist Ludwig Eichrodt. Biedermeier furniture and decorative arts, with their solid, *gemütlich* elegance, came to symbolize

OPPOSITE: *T*hanks to the technical perfection increasingly brought to the piano, this instrument became an obligatory piece of furniture in the parlors of bourgeois Europe, beginning in the early nineteenth century. ABOVE: Lithographic portrait of Franz Schubert by Josef Kriehuber.

the virtues and aspirations of Vienna's bourgeoisie, a vital force opportunistically risen to power in place of a decadent aristocracy ruined by the Napoleonic wars and the extravagance of their social life during the Congress of Vienna. Although adapted from the high, Neoclassical formality of the Empire style, Biedermeier furniture was generally arranged in an easy, asymmetrical manner, its appeal largely dependent upon the colors of the woods or the subtle variety of the materials used. In Biedermeier, the Empire style may have lost its ormolu and gilding, but the sobriety and refinement remained, along with the easy grace, comfort, and conviviality for which Biedermeier is famous. The wall fabrics, with their simple motifs and soft col-

ors, are light and luminous. Also essential to the décor was an abundance of watercolors and oils representing scenes of domestic life or beautiful landscapes. The parlor, a gathering place for family and friends, played a major role in the Biedermeier household.

ABOVE: *The inner courtyard of the "Red Crayfish House," where Schubert was born. The family lived upstairs, above the school run by the future composer's father. Franz, too, would earn his living as a school teacher.* RIGHT: *A nook in the old kitchen.*

Here, usually, were to be found musical instruments and beautiful music stands, the latter sometimes specially designed for quartet playing.

It was in this kind of salon that the "Schuberti-ads" took place, those musical events during which the composer arranged performances of his *lieder* and chamber pieces for the pleasure of friends or admir-ers. The scene is wonderfully evoked in *A Schubert Evening at Joseph von Spaun's*, the famous drawing by Schubert's great friend, the witty Moritz von Schwind, perhaps the most Biedermeier of all painters. Around the piano, played by four hands, is gathered an audi-ence of some fifty attentive people. Occasionally the Schubertiads took place in a Viennese café, such as the "Green Anchor Inn" *(Zum Grünen Anker)* next to St. Ste-phen's, or even at a friendly tavern in the countryside around Vienna.

The success of these amiable moments did not carry over into the economic sphere. Unable or unwill-ing to promote his talents within the musical estab-lishment, Schubert never succeeded in living by his art and often had to make do with a meager school-teacher's salary. If not at home with his parents, the composer had to share a room with a friend, as in 1818, when he stayed at a boarding house run by Frau Sans-souci in Wipplingerstrasse near the old Town Hall. From his roommate, the poet Johann Mayrhofer, we have a description of this charmless place: "The house and the room had undergone the vicissitudes of the age; the ceiling was low, the light inadequate, blocked by a large building next door; a miserable piano [Schubert had yet to move in], a narrow bookcase. . . ."

Very similar must have been the other poverty-stricken student lodgings inhabited by young Schubert either alone or with some friend. In addition to his sojourns with the Schobers, the summer months some-times allowed him to escape the wretchedness of his normal environment. Thus, in 1818 and again in 1824, he found employment with Count Johann Karl Ester-házy and his family, a distant branch of Haydn's Ester-házys, and accompanied them to their estate at Schloss Zseliz in Hungary, where he served as musical tutor to his employer's children. Even while living in the out-buildings and eating with the servants, Schubert ap-pears to have enjoyed the pleasures of country life.

In 1819, 1823, and 1825 Schubert traveled to Steyr and Salzkammergut with the baritone Michael Vogl, one of the first to recognize the genius of his ac-companist. In both places the two artists were warmly received, as a result of which the Schubertiads found their way into Upper Austria. Their friend Stylvester Paumgartner made music the overriding priority of his life. According to Albert Stadler, a Schubert disci-ple at the Stadtkonvikt but a native of Steyr, "Paum-gartner lived alone in his house, without tenants. The upper story was his habitat and the place of his music room, furnished for practice during the day and inti-mate parties in the evening. Upstairs was a parlor deco-rated with representations of all the arts and meant for the frequent and important small concerts given for afternoon visits." It was thanks to a commission

ABOVE: *The inner courtyard at the house of Franz Schubert's brother Ferdinand, a brilliant pedagogue but a mediocre com-poser. It was here that Schubert died on 19 November 1828.*

formed in public, which meant that he built no reputation as a virtuoso pianist, unlike Mozart or Beethoven. Also, in an era when the taste for opera—especially Italian opera—reigned supreme, Schubert was never at his best in lyric drama, despite many attempts at the genre. Then, too, there was destiny, which denied him the time in which to achieve great public acclaim, despite his catalogue of more than a thousand compositions.

At the beginning of 1823, Franz Schubert fell gravely ill and did not recover, however provisionally, until the end of the year. Failing health, caused by venereal infection, may explain why he never finished the famous *"Unfinished" Symphony* (No. 7, Symphony in C minor), a work not discovered and performed until 1865. At the time of his fourth stay with the Schobers, beginning in March 1827, Schubert found an outlet for his physical and moral state in the pathetic, visionary song cycle known as *Winterreise (Winter Journey)*. Early in September 1828 Schubert, on the advice of his doctor, left central Vienna and moved in—temporarily he thought—with his brother Ferdinand at Kettenbrückengasse 6, then a suburb of the capital. There he contracted typhoid fever and died on 19 November. He was only thirty-two.

The night before he died, the half-conscious Schubert asked his brother: "Do I not deserve a place on the face of the earth?"

from Paumgartner that Schubert composed the *Trout Quintet,* its theme drawn from an original melody written two years earlier.

One might well ask why the admiration aroused by Schubert within his circles of cultivated amateurs did not spread to the larger world of music lovers. Surely the composer's modesty and shyness were not the sole reasons. True enough, Schubert never per-

ABOVE: *The corridor in the house of Schubert's brother Ferdinand.* OPPOSITE: *Ferdinand's piano, on which Schubert, in September 1828, very likely composed his* later works for the instrument: *Piano Sonatas No. 17 in C minor, No. 18 in A, and No. 19 in B flat. The bust of the composer is by Joseph Alois Dialer.*

Hector
Berlioz
1803–1869

No one ever evoked his own country more vividly than Hector Berlioz, a composer who also happened to be a gifted writer: "I was born on 11 December 1803 at La Côte-Saint-André, a small village in France located in the Isère Department, between Vienne, Grenoble, and Lyons. . . . La Côte-Saint-André, as its name suggests, is built on the side of a hill, overlooking a vast plain—rich, golden, verdant—whose silence resonates a kind of marvelous, dreamy majesty, made all the more so by the ring of mountains circling about on both the south and the east, and beyond which in the distance loom the gigantic, glacier-clad peaks of the Alps."

Berlioz belonged to a family of tanners long established in the Dauphiné, where, during the eighteenth century, they had steadily risen in social rank. Their success is reflected in the dining room of the house where Berlioz came into the world, a space dominated by the portrait of the composer's grandfather, Louis-Joseph Berlioz, a majestic, self-satisfied presence attired in the black robe of an attorney at the audit court for the Dauphiné. Louis Berlioz, Hector's father, was a medical doctor, who, as Hector put it, "inspired great confidence, not only in our small town but also in neighboring towns." The Côte-Saint-André house, so typical of a provincial eminence, reflected less the size of the doctor's practice, carried on by a man noted for his charity, than the grandeur of his inheritance—properties, farms, and fields—all of which made Louis Berlioz the town's second most important landlord.

The residence, with its austere façade, reveals a certain moneyed charm as soon as one has set foot in the porte-cochère. This leads into a courtyard surrounded on three sides by the house's main wings, disposed in U-formation, vine-covered, and hung with a wooden balcony running completely about. One enters the house down a brief flight of stairs in a large vestibule, which gives access to the medical office and the kitchen, with its heavy beams, ruddy floor tiles,

and monumental fireplace. Upstairs is the parlor floor, divided into a large parlor, a dining room, and the master bedroom. On the next floor above are the other bedrooms.

It was from Louis Berlioz himself that Hector received his first music lessons. They began after the boy discovered an old flageolet at the back of a drawer and made "a futile effort to render the popular Marlborough song." The pathetic piping so annoyed Dr. Berlioz that he thought it better to teach his son how to play the instrument. Hector proved extraordinarily adept: "After seven or eight months," wrote the mature composer, "I had become a flautist of passable talent." This musical progress no doubt took place in the main parlor, an elegant room boasting herringbone parquet, sober furniture, and the young prodigy's mahogany music stand.

OPPOSITE: *View from the small parlor to the large one in the home of Dr. Louis Berlioz. It was here that the physician gave his son lessons "in languages, literature, history, geography, and even music." On the far wall hangs the portrait of Espérance Robert, the composer's grandmother.*
ABOVE: *Portrait of Hector Berlioz, a Prix de Rome winner, painted by Claude-Marie Dubufe.*

Dr. Berlioz arranged for a musician named Imbert to come from Lyons and "teach both instrumental and vocal music to a dozen of the village schoolchildren for a fee of eight francs per month." Needless to say, Hector counted among the chosen few. When Imbert left La Côte-Saint-André, following the suicide of his own son, he was replaced by an Alsatian named Dorant. Hector wasted no time mastering "those three majestic and incomparable instruments, the flageolet,

"*L*a Côte-Saint-André, a French village, situated in the Isère Department . . . is built on the side of a hill, overlooking a vast plain—rich, golden, verdant—whose silence resonates a kind of marvelous, dreamy majesty, made all the more so by the ring of mountains circling about on both the south and the east, and beyond which in the distance loom the gigantic, glacier-clad peaks of the Alps."

the flute, and the guitar." Meanwhile, curiosity drove him still further. Rummaging about in the library, he discovered a copy of Rameau's *Treatise on Harmony,* "annotated and simplified by d'Alembert." Thereupon he "spent whole nights reading these obscure theories, without making any sense of them." Undiscouraged nonetheless, he commenced, at the age of twelve and a half, his career in musical composition, the first fruits of which were a six-part pot-pourri on Italian airs and, more important, two quintets for flute, two violins, alto, and bass. The first quintet won plaudits from the local amateurs who performed it; the second less so, owing to its greater difficulty. In 1826, however, Berlioz reused a passage in the *Francs-Juges* overture: "the song in A flat, carried by the first violins, right after the beginning of the allegro."

Still, the Berlioz household was not a family of passionate music lovers like that of, say, Felix Mendelssohn. Note, for instance, the absence of a piano, already a feature virtually de rigueur in bourgeois parlors. The two pianos now in the house are a pianoforte of unknown origin installed in recent times and an 1858 Érard given by the composer to his niece Adèle. In truth, Louis Berlioz viewed music as little more than a hobby, and when Hector left for Paris in 1821 it was with instructions that he enroll in medical school and forget the idea of becoming a professional musician. As for his mother, "whose religious opinions ran to great exaltation," she believed that "actors, actresses, singers, musicians, poets, and composers were abominable creatures, excommunicated by the Church and thus predestined for Hell."

Despite this, it was during his first eighteen years in La Côte-Saint-André that Hector Berlioz developed the most important and essential elements of his personality: the love of wind instruments, inherited from that first flageolet; the feeling for religious music, revealed to him, as the composer wrote in his *Mémoires,* at the time of his first communion (one thinks of *L'Enfance du Christ*); the sense of nature (the oboe in *Harold en Italie* sounds more Cisalpine than Transalpine); and also the stubborn, romantic pursuit of an impossible love.

As for the last, it was near Grenoble, some fifty kilometers from La Côte-Saint-André, that young Hec-

tor discovered his capacity for all-consuming love. In the village of Meyland, Hector's grandparents owned a house where the family spent part of every summer. Nearby lived a Mme Gautier, "who during the high season stayed there together with her two nieces, the younger of whom was named Estelle." Estelle Duboeuf was eighteen, whereas Hector was only twelve: "As soon as I saw her I felt an electric shock; I loved her, quite

In his Mémoires, Berlioz, who lived to recall the difficulties of his life, made no mention of the comfortable existence his family had come to enjoy, thanks to their enterprise but *also to their beneficial alliances, all of which is reflected in this peaceful and well-appointed house. OVERLEAF: The spacious provincial kitchen.*

simply. I was overcome by dizziness and remained that way. . . . I spent whole nights in a state of desolation. By day I hid out in corn fields, in the secret recesses of my grandfather's orchard, like a wounded bird, mute with suffering."

Back in La Côte-Saint-André, the love-sick Hector remained inconsolable. He even broke down at school during an explication of Dido's death in the fourth canto of the *Aeneid*. Forty years later, in 1856, Berlioz was to recall the incident as he launched into the composition of *Les Troyens*. Estelle would also inspire the "Rêveries, Passions" episode in the *Symphonie fantastique*, not to mention several other works.

"No, time did not heal . . . other loves did not efface the memory of the first." Berlioz would forever be haunted by his youth in the Dauphiné. In 1832 he stopped at La Côte-Saint-André following his return from the Villa Medici, where his Prix de Rome had allowed him to spend most of 1831 and 1832. Continuing on to Meylan, he secretly spied on Estelle, now "Mme F," and returned home "quivering with commotion." Again, in 1848, he returned to his native village, this time following the death of his father, and once more he attempted to catch a glimpse of Estelle. To no avail, for she now lived in Vif, about fifteen kilometers south of Grenoble. "I still love her," Berlioz declared to his cousin Victor. "But imbecile," exploded Victor, "she is now fifty-one years old!" Undeterred, the composer wrote Estelle a wonderful and heart-breaking love letter, to which no reply ever came.

Berlioz persisted, and in 1854, having found the address of Mme F, he went, with fluttering heart, to call on his "Stella." Thereupon they began a correspondence which takes up the last part of the composer's *Mémoires.* Finally, in August 1865, Berlioz returned to the Dauphiné and then went on to Geneva for a meeting with Estelle, to whom he proposed marriage, a half-century after their first encounter. She refused him.

Hector Berlioz died on 8 March 1869, having survived two wives and a great love.

OPPOSITE: *On a dining-room wall in the Berlioz family home the portrait of Louis-Joseph Berlioz (1747–1815), the composer's grandfather and the family's first man of distinction. The eighteenth-century wall painting has only recently been rediscovered.*

ABOVE: *Hector Berlioz's bedroom.* OVERLEAF: *The large parlor in the Berlioz family home in the Dauphiné, furnished with the young composer's double music stand fashioned of mahogany.*

Ole
Bull
1810–1880

A virtuoso equal to Paganini, as well as a widely acclaimed composer, Ole Bull was one of the most astounding personalities of the Romantic century. He even appeared, occasionally, on the same bill with Mendelssohn and Adelina Patti, winning the admiration of Schumann, Mark Twain, Longfellow, Thackeray, and Shaw. His friends included Liszt, Grieg, and La Malibran. George Sand took Ole Bull as a model for the hero of her novel *Malgré tout*, while Ibsen, another intimate, borrowed certain of the master's characteristics for Peer Gynt.

Today Ole Bull has been largely forgotten, and not altogether unjustly. In Norway, though, he remains what has been conveniently called an "emblematic" figure. Like Sibelius in Finland a bit later, Bull emerged as the first international celebrity to symbolize the political independence of his country, a nation proud of its own language and culture.

Bull was born in Bergen on 5 February 1810. By the age of five he could hold a violin; by eight he had taken his place in the family quartet; and at nine he was performing as a soloist with the Bergen Philharmonic. Further, Bull was only eighteen when he first conducted the municipal-theatre orchestra, then the most important in Norway. By adolescence he had already proved his originality, and save for his failure to pass the entrance examination at the Bergen seminary, he might very well have become a pastor as well as a musician.

Meanwhile, the prodigy studied with local disciples of Giovanni Viotti and Pierre Baillot, even as he was profiting from the example of such country fiddlers as Torgeir Augundson, famous throughout Norway as *Møllerguten* ("Miller's Lads"), who taught him their folk dances: the *slåtter*. Folklore would in fact provide Bull with important themes for several of his works, as well as for the modifications he made to his instrument. Inspired by the mountaineer fiddlers of

Hardanger, whose rural violins have underlying sympathetic drone strings, Bull adopted a flatter bridge and a more curved bow, thereby reviving a Baroque tradition that today is again in vogue, a century and a half after the great Norwegian's experiments.

The nonconformist Bull went on to have a truly brilliant career. Welcomed throughout Europe, he gave as many as two hundred concerts a year, becoming a true musical ambassador for a Norway liberated only in 1814 from the secular hegemony of Denmark. Significantly enough, he based one of his first major compositions, *Hymne to Freedom* (1829), on a text by the Norwegian poet Henrik Wergeland. Yet, at the same time he produced such nationalist pieces as *Souvenirs de Norvège* (later known as *The Mountains of Norway*), a work for country fiddle, string quartet, flute,

*T*he summer house built by Ole Bull, a personality quite out of the ordinary, could only be extraordinary. His "Little Alhambra," a Moorish fantasy in faun-colored wood, stands tall above the densely forested landscape of a Norwegian fjord. ABOVE: *Photographic portrait of Ole Bull, before 1880.*

The "Little Alhambra" of Lysøen

and bass violin, Bull was also making his music a road map of his travels: *Recitativo, adagio amorosa* [sic] *con polacca guerriera*, inspired by an eruption of Vesuvius; *Concerto irlandais* (*Farewell to Ireland*); *Homage to Edinburgh* (also *Scottish Concerto*); *Hommage à Moscou, Carnaval de Venise*, etc.

Inevitably, the adventurous Bull would be drawn to the United States, along with legions of other Euro-

"*I* had a very pleasant little party-kin last night at Cambridge at Longfellow's, where there was a mad-cap fiddler Ole Bull, who played most wonderfully on his instrument, and charmed me still more by his oddities and character. Quite a character for a book." *William Makepeace Thackeray* (1855).

pean artists then embarking westward. His first American tour occurred in 1843, during which he became something of an "adopted son." Only in 1845 did he return to Europe, this time touring all the way to Algeria, a land still *terra incognita* to contemporary Europeans. Arriving in Naples, Bull learned of the 1848 revolution that had erupted in virtually every European capital. The news sent him scurrying to Paris in the hope of making common cause, on behalf of the Norwegian people, with another republican hero of the Romantic era: the poet Alphonse Lamartine. Later in the year, on 10 December, Bull found himself hailed in triumph by the students of Bergen. For the occasion, he had composed a fantasy, *Et Sæterbesøg (Visit to the Sæter)*, even today a great popular favorite among Norwegians. A few months later, Bull founded Norway's first national theatre, locating it in Bergen. In 1851, he recruited as director a largely unknown twenty-three-year-old playwright named Henrik Ibsen.

Rikard Nordraak, a talented but short-lived Norwegian composer, so revered Ole Bull that he even collected the master's cigar butts, as if they were holy relics. The musician did indeed have a mesmerizing effect on his contemporaries, thanks in considerable part to the almost epic saga of his life. Among the legendary episodes was an attempt to establish a Norwegian colony in the Pennsylvania wilderness. There was also that horseback journey made as part of a successful campaign to persuade the Grieg family that young Edvard should be allowed to pursue a musical career. In a no less flamboyant gesture he kept his promise to perform *Et Sæterbesøg* on top of Egypt's Pyramid of Cheops, doing so on his sixty-sixth birthday!

In 1836 Ole Bull had married a Frenchwoman, Félicie Villeminot, who died in 1862. In 1870 he took a second wife, Sarah Thorp, daughter of an American Senator and forty years younger than her husband. Bull now divided his life between Wisconsin and Norway, with the latter preferred in summer. For this he chose a 170-acre domain on Lysøen—one of the country's 5,000 islands—located in a fjord south of Bergen. Leaving intact the old farm buildings, once the property of a Cistercian monastery, he initiated construction on a nearby hillside, a project undertaken by the architect Conrad Frederik von der Lippe and a

local carpenter, the master builder Ingebrigt Bøe. Bull set a tight budget for the project, but for the want of economy among his many virtues, he ended up having to make several concert tours before all the bills could be paid.

What came forth on tiny Lysøen Island startles even today, even those sensitive to the originality of the person responsible. Here, at a latitude of 60 degrees north, several thousand kilometers from Granada,

"If Ole Bull had been born without arms, what a rank he would have taken among the poets—because it is in him, & if he couldn't violin it out, he would talk it out, since of course it would have to come out." Mark Twain (1880).

stands an extravagant Moorish palace, complete with ogives and openwork arches, the whole crowned by a sort of onion-domed bell tower and inevitably known the "Little Alhambra." Meandering, sand-covered paths guide strollers through the woods during the long white nights of the Norwegian summer. Bull erected piers, fountains, and summer houses, planted orchards, and even assumed the challenge of cultivating flowers with exotic perfumes. At the bottom of the curving entrance stairs one can almost see the passionate violinist just as he appears in an 1880 photograph—a character from a Western, wearing a broad-brimmed hat and a double chain swagged across his vest.

Even more spectacular than the exterior is the blond-wood interior, an extravaganza of Norwegian "stave-church" functionality and Islamic elaborations. Almost the whole of the principal floor is given over to one central room, a music salon large enough to hold as many as a hundred people, all seated. Paired rows of twisted columns support a filigreed vault which even the Omayyads would not have scorned. Huge Murano chandeliers illuminate the nave-like space at night, while by day sunlight pours in through tall ogive windows. Oriental carpets cover the floor, while other souvenirs of a triumphal career abound on every side. Here Ole Bull made his violins sing—an Amati, a Stradivarius, a Gasparo da Salò, and the traditional Hardanger—for the pleasure of his family, his friends, and even the farmers and other folk of the neighboring countryside.

Ole Bull spent his last eighteen summers in his "Little Alhambra" on Lysøen. He died there on 17 August 1880, following his return from yet another American tour. Grieg, who owed him so much, delivered the eulogy at the master's funeral, citing "the pioneer of our national music, beloved beyond all others, warm, and loyal."

LEFT: *Ole Bull's bedroom in the "Little Alhambra."*
OPPOSITE: *The music salon (detail). Ole Bull not only brought great innovations to the violin; he also collaborated with an American engineer,* *John Ericsson, to improve the piano. The instrument, emblazoned with the musician's name, was inaugurated at a concert played by the great pianist (and composer) Agathe Backer-Grøndalh.*

Frédéric
Chopin
1810–1849

"What an unsympathetic woman that Sand! Is she really a woman? I'm prepared to doubt it." Such was the reaction of Frédéric Chopin following his first encounter with George Sand in October 1838. The future lovers had just been introduced at a dinner in the home of Franz Liszt and his mistress, Countess Marie d'Agoult.

Born at Zelazowa Wola, near Warsaw, on 1 March 1810, Chopin was the son of a French tutor and his Polish wife, Justyna Krzyzanowska, both of them good amateur musicians and both in service to the same aristocratic family. Frédéric—a child prodigy who at eighteen had already compiled a catalogue of some fifty original compositions—made his first appearance in Paris during the autumn of 1831. He was well received from the start, less for his talents as a concert pianist than for his compositional gift or even for his teaching.

George Sand, six years older than Chopin, was already wildly famous, thanks not only to her romantic novels, among them *Indiana, Valentine,* and *Jacques,* but also to her tumultuous amours with the likes of Jules Sandeau, Prosper Mérimée, and Alfred de Musset. Adding to the aura of notoriety was her habit of wearing male attire and smoking a pipe or cigar in public. Even so, Chopin waited no more than a few days before inviting Sand to the inauguration of his new Paris apartment at 38 Rue de la Chaussée d'Antin. Over the next several months their friendship grew increasingly intimate, despite the formal courtship the pianist had long been paying to a sixteen-year-old Polish girl, Maria Wodzinska. Parental consent, however, had become ever

"*Like her, he manages racket and chatter, fright and delight, a gift even more subtle because of Mme Sand, who, as woman and poet, is entitled twice over, thanks to the intuition of her heart and to her genius.*" Franz Liszt, Chopin (1852).

OPPOSITE: *George Sand's bedroom at Nohant.*
ABOVE: *Frédéric Chopin, photographed by L. Bisson (1849).*

Life with George Sand at Nohant

"At any moment in the garden, gusts of music may come through the window where Chopin works at [George's] side; it blends with the roses and the song of nightingales." Eugène Delacroix, Correspondance. Matthew Arnold described Nohant as *"a plain house by the roadside with a walled garden."*

more doubtful. One vexing problem was Chopin's delicate health, which, in February 1837, had entered a critical stage. Too, the proper Polish family may have been shocked by the company Chopin chose to keep in Paris, a society tolerant of "lost women" like Marie d'Agoult and George Sand. Come the following August, the engagement would be called off.

On 20 May 1838 George Sand wrote to a friend that she and Chopin had succumbed to the inevitable: "We did not deny one another; we let ourselves be car-

ried away by the passing wind, both of us transported into another realm for a few moments. But in the wake of that celestial fire, we must nonetheless came back to earth." In November the lovers departed for Majorca, along with Sand's two children: fifteen-year-old Maurice and ten-year-old Solange. While on Majorca, Chopin overcame his deteriorating health to compose one of his greatest masterpieces, the cycle of twenty-four Preludes. The Prelude in D flat major (No. 5), which evokes a cascading drop of water, may very well

have been inspired by the rain which fell throughout the winter. Sand and Chopin did not return to France until the spring of 1839. Following a brief interlude in Italy, they traveled directly from Marseilles to Nohant, Sand's estate in Berry. The couple arrived there on 1 June.

The Château de Nohant—actually a large manor house—had been constructed in the 1770s by the governor of Vierzon, who sold it in 1793 to Sand's grandmother, Marie-Aurore Dupin de Francueil, the natural daughter of the famous Maréchal de Saxe, himself the bastard son of a Polish King! George Sand—legally the estranged wife of Baron Casimir Dudevant—had inherited the property in 1821.

Nohant lay approximately 300 kilometers from Paris, or 30 hours as the mail coach traveled. Just outside the château's main gate are the village's rustic square and small Romanesque church. Behind the simple three-story dwelling spreads an ample park, complete with formal French garden, a kitchen garden, a small, shaggy wood, and the family cemetery. While the exterior of the house is rather ordinary, the interior offers many charms, its furniture and decoration a mélange of things inherited from Mme Dupin and others introduced by Sand. Apart from the salon and the boudoir, both a bit overcrowded with mismatched pieces, the most important rooms on the ground floor are the dining room, the kitchen, and the parlor in which Chopin installed his piano.

George Sand, ever sensitive to Chopin's needs, had Camille Pleyel send a piano of just the right size. The novelist described how Chopin, secure in his music room, composed while "pacing up and down, breaking his pens, singing, and altering every measure a hundred times." No matter, the list of the works Chopin created at Nohant is impressive: the Sonata in B flat minor (the "Funeral"), the Sonata in B minor; seven Nocturnes, the third and fourth Ballades, the third and fourth Scherzos, some fifteen Mazurkas, the Fantasy Polonaise in A flat major, and several other pieces.

The handsome dining room, like the immense kitchen with its monumental hearth and pâtisserie oven, bears witness to the dedication with which Sand, the author of *Autour de la table*, nurtured the conviviality of her household. And Nohant never lacked for

"I have endless tête-à-têtes with Chopin, whom I very much like and who is a man of rare distinction. He is the truest artist I have ever met. He is among the very few whom one can admire and esteem." Eugène Delacroix, Correspondance.

I was made to dine. The food is good, but there is too much game and chicken, which disagrees with me. Also present were the painter Marchal,

Alexandre Dumas fils, Mme Calamatta." Théophile Gautier, as recorded by the Goncourts, Journal (14 September 1863).

guests to enjoy it, everyone from simple neighbors, such as the good Dr. Gustave Papet, who gave Chopin every care, to visiting Poles. Celebrities came in droves, among them Franz Liszt, Honoré de Balzac, the reclusive Flaubert, and Pauline Viardot, the sister of La Malibran and a celebrated singer in her own right. Eugène Delacroix was such a frequent guest that he set up a studio at Nohant, declaring his "convent life" there to be entirely agreeable.

Summer days at Nohant, with its "monotone, sweet, and tranquil" life, gave Chopin deep pleasure, just as it did Sand, who wrote of the daily regimen: "My tutorial for Maurice and Solange continues day in and day out, even on Sunday from noon until five o'clock. We dine alfresco, friends arrive, first one and then another; we smoke, we chatter away, and in the evening, when everyone has left, Chopin goes to the

piano and, between dog and wolf, plays for me, after which he retires, sleeping like a babe, at the same time as Maurice and Solange. Meanwhile, I read the *Encyclopédie* and prepare my lesson for tomorrow." As this letter of 1839 reveals, the two lovers did not keep the same schedule. Upstairs, furthermore, their rooms were adjacent but nonetheless separate. This allowed Sand to work late, sometimes until dawn, writing countless long letters as well as articles, plays, and the twenty odd novels she published during the period, including *Le Compagnon du tour de France, Consuelo, Fanchette,* and *La Mare au diable.*

Chopin, in all, spent seven summers at Nohant, the first in 1839 and the last in 1846. Midway through autumn, the couple always returned to Paris, Chopin frequently sooner than Sand. In 1842 the composer moved into the ground-floor flat at 9 Square d'Orléans,

not far from the Trinité Church and his earlier domiciles, in that Right Bank quarter favored by writers and artists identified with the Nouvelle Athènes café. George Sand, meanwhile, took a lease on the main floor at 5 Square d'Orléans. Chopin, more and more weakened by tuberculosis, went on giving music lessons and a few private concerts, but he almost never made a public appearance. By the end of spring, or sometimes earlier, the Sand/Chopin ménage would again set out for Nohant.

During the summer of 1844, however, the peaceful, family-like atmosphere of Nohant began to disintegrate. On 15 October of that year Sand wrote to a friend: "On bright days [Chopin] is cheerful, but when it rains he turns gloomy, bored to death. He takes no pleasure in what I do and enjoy in the country. . . ." The children having now grown up, the tight little

community found itself beset by cross-currents of internecine rivalry. Maurice, who sided with his mother, loathed Solange, who succeeded in getting Chopin to take her part. A further complication was the composer's Polish manservant, Jan, who suddenly managed to offend everyone, thereby precipitating his own dismissal. To make matters worse, Sand decided to adopt a young cousin, Augustine Brault, who could not resist flirting with Maurice, a development which further poisoned the atmosphere. In 1847 Sand began to suspect

—no doubt incorrectly—an affair between Solange, then nineteen, and Chopin, who that summer did not return to Nohant. On 28 July he wrote Sand a letter which concluded with these words: "Time will heal. I shall wait—*still* the same. Your ever devoted friend. Chopin." He and George Sand would meet only one more time, and this by chance, in March 1848. Eight months later, on 17 October 1849, Frédéric Chopin died in Paris.

At Nohant, Eugène Delacroix had painted Chopin improvising on the piano, with an attentive George Sand seated comfortably behind him. The picture, unfinished though wonderful, was cut in half by an owner whose name deserves oblivion. Today the image of Chopin hangs in the Louvre, while that of Sand adorns the Ordrupgård Museum near Copenhagen.

The kitchens are among the most remarkable rooms in the Château de Nohant, a place resonant with memories of George Sand and Frédéric Chopin. Nohant, located in deepest Berry, has now been tastefully restored by France's Caisse Nationale des Monuments Historiques et des Sites.

Franz
Liszt
1811–1886

It is to Franz Liszt that we owe the recital, not only as a concept but also as a word, which he introduced on 9 June 1840 at a concert in London: "I have dared to give a series of concerts featuring myself alone, imitating Louis XIV and announcing to the world: *'Le Concert, c'est moi!'*" Born in 1811 in Raiding, Hungary, Liszt made his debut in October 1820 at the age of nine. During the early 1830s he emerged as the prototype of the great international pianist, an artistic phenomenon now quite familiar. During what he called his *Glanzperiode*—his time of splendor—Liszt toured the whole of Europe, from Lisbon to Constantinople and from St. Petersburg to Rome, everywhere hysterically acclaimed, adulated, and plied with both gold and women.

Meanwhile, there was another Liszt, a man whom such a career, however brilliant, could not entirely satisfy—a person of fervor and reflection who cried: "Always concerts! Always a servant to the public! . . . What a profession!" By February 1848 the great virtuoso had decided to settle in Weimar, a Gothic/Rococo village dominated by an immense onion-domed castle, the whole once described by Mme de Staël less "a town than an overgrown château." Liszt had already given

several series of concerts at Weimar and even been named honorary Kapellmeister by the young Grand Duke Carl Alexander. Along with the title came a warm invitation to join the court for good, an offer Liszt finally accepted for several evident reasons. The tiny duchy, with a population of just over 13,000 souls, enjoyed such cultural distinction that it was known as "the Athens of the North." Johann Sebastian Bach had worked there from 1707 to 1718, the period of his famous *Brandenburg Concertos*. Until 1830 Johann Nepomuk Hummel, one of the finest pianists of his time as well as a notable composer, had once held the position whose duties Liszt would now assume. Further adding to Weimar's lustre were the many outstanding writers—Wieland, Herder, Schiller, and Goethe among them—who had lived and worked there.

When Franz Liszt settled in Weimar in 1848, he lived first at the Hotel Erbprinz. Two years later he and Carolyne von Sayn-Wittengenstein moved into the Altenburg. Beginning in 1869, the composer would stay alone in the more modest surroundings of the Hofgärtnerei.
LEFT AND OPPOSITE: *The entrance door and the garden at the Hofgärtnerei.*
ABOVE: *Portrait of Franz Liszt by Kriehuber (1856).*

In Weimar

Another reason was Liszt's desire to reside in peace with Princess Carolyne von Sayn-Wittgenstein, the wealthy Polish aristocrat who for the last several months had taken the place held by Countess Marie d'Agoult from 1833 to 1844. Too, Weimar represented an island of calm in a Europe everywhere afflicted by revolutionary troubles. In sum, Liszt could hardly have found a more perfect environment in which to realize his dream, which was "to escape the trap of virtuosity and let my mind take flight."

Franz Liszt would spend thirteen years in Weimar, where he took possession of a large house, the Altenburg, on an eponymous hill situated about a kilo-

meter from the town center. Isolated and surrounded by woods, the dwelling provided a magnificent view over Weimar. At first Liszt rented the property from one Ulysses Stock, who, seeing a chance to profit, set about constructing next door an open-air dance hall sure to attract all those curious about the famous person in their midst. The dowager Grand Duchess saved the day by purchasing the property and offering it in "grace and favor" to her prize musician.

At Altenburg the piano reigned supreme, with no less than seven instruments scattered about the house: a concert grand Boisselot in the blue study next to Liszt's bedroom; Beethoven's Broadwood in another room; in the main salon the Érard formerly used by the virtuoso; and, finally, in the music room a Streicher, a Bösendorfer, a spinet once owned by Mozart, and a gigantic "piano-organ" with three manuals, six registers, and a pedal board. Spread throughout the house were, of course, the furniture, rugs, malachite objects, silver-dipped laurel wreaths, and other costly souvenirs

"It is the generous chord that he makes vibrate most of all. He also attacks the angry note, but never the hateful one." George Sand, Journal de Piffoël. *ABOVE: The music room at the*

Hofgärtnerei. The house has now become a museum dedicated to the composer.
OPPOSITE: *Bust of Franz Liszt by the sculptor Lorenzo Bartolini (1838).*

"Liszt, who lived at Weimar in a princely house, became the center of a constellation of more or less extravagant composers, among whom must be cited Wagner, Schumann, Raff, Bülow, Joachim. . . ." Oscar Comettant, Musique et Musiciens (1862).

accumulated during countless tours—all mingled together with such cherished relics as Beethoven's death mask, a secretary once owned by Haydn, and precious music manuscripts. The large library bore witness to its owner's vast intellectual scope. At Altenburg, Liszt not only produced some 700 scores; he also wrote a number of books, two of them—*Frédéric Chopin* and *The Gypsies and Their Music in Hungary*—at Altenburg.

Carolyne von Wittgenstein and her daughter Marie had special apartments. In addition, Altenburg housed five servants (one of them a magician), Rappo the dog, and a cat named Mme Esmeralda. The mansion was also constantly filled with visitors: Joachim Raff, Liszt's secretary and a talented composer to boot; numerous Weimar regulars; and artists as well as friends passing through. Wagner, fleeing the police after his involvement in the Dresden uprising of 1849, found refuge at Altenburg. Liszt received nothing from the Weimar court—his Kapellmeister title being honorary —and Princess Carolyne kept a tight rein on her fortune; still, the composer extended hospitality with his usual open-handed generosity.

A young American pianist, William Mason, spent sixteen months in Weimar, where he found the kindest possible reception at Altenburg. According to his in-valuable diary, soirées on the hilltop were both continuous and extremely varied. For 4 June 1853 there is this entry: "In the evening we were all invited to the Altenburg. [Liszt] played 'Harmonies du soir, No. 2' and his own sonata. He was at his best and played divinely." A few days later, on 10 June, Mason noted: "Went to Liszt's this evening to a bock-beer soirée. The beer was a present to Liszt from Pruchner's father who has a large brewery in Munich."

As Liszt had hoped, Weimar allowed his mind to take flight. As a result, he composed a number of important masterpieces, including the Sonata in B minor, the *Faust Symphony* and most of the symphonic poems, the oratorio *Christus*, the organ fantasy and fugue on the chorale *Ad nos, ad salutarem undam*, etc.

And this was not the whole of the great man's accomplishment at Altenburg. Liszt also taught piano, composition, and singing, free of charge. He took under his wing such gifted young musicians as Hans von Bülow, who in 1857 married Cosima, one of the

three daughters the composer had with Marie d'Agoult. Little did either Liszt or von Bülow imagine that one day Cosima would fall into the arms of Richard Wagner. For more than a decade Liszt was the indefatigable engine of cultural life in Weimar. To the Hoftheatre he brought the greatest performers of the age as well as the world premiere of Wagner's *Lohengrin* and the first local production of Verdi's *Ernani*. He organized several "Berlioz Weeks" and championed the works of many other composers. Liszt established both a foundation and a festival dedicated to Goethe, in addition to a

sort of academy, the Neu Weimar Verein, which attracted to the duchy such writers as England's George Eliot and Denmark's Hans Christian Andersen.

Life at Weimar, however, was not without its trials, as one biographer made clear in a chapter entitled "A Giant in Lilliput." The theatre was inadequately funded, making every production a tour de force that sometimes proved beyond even the powers of Liszt. For this, the ever-present gaggle of mediocrities and jealous individuals blamed the supposed luxury of Altenburg, where, in any event, the lifestyle was not supported by public money. The small town fairly buzzed with gossip, almost invariably without basis.

Still more painful was "good" society's ostracism of Carolyne von Wittgenstein, reproached for living with Liszt before her divorce had become final, for dressing in too lavish a manner, and for smoking huge cigars in public. Finally, Liszt and the Princess, both of them Catholic, came to feel uncomfortable in a largely Protestant community, one that viewed "papists" with suspicion. As a consequence, direct or indirect, Liszt rediscovered his faith, which had somewhat cooled during the *Glanzperiode*.

The petty snubs proving unbearable, Liszt, from 1855 onward, performed more and more elsewhere, in Vienna, Paris, Dresden, Prague, etc. In Germany and the Austrian Empire, however, he found himself confronted by growing hostility to the "music of the future," i.e., the compositions of Liszt and Wagner. In June 1859 Grand Duchess Maria Pavlovna died. In May of the following year Carolyne von Wittgenstein left for Rome, in the hope of having the Russian civil annulment of her marriage confirmed by the Papal court. On 12 August 1861 Liszt followed her, leaving Altenburg forever.

In 1869, however, Liszt somewhat resumed his musical activity in Weimar, where he visited several times before his death on 31 July 1886. On these occasions he lived more modestly, at the so-called *Hofgärtnerei* ("House of the Court Gardener") but in fact the former studio of the painter Friedrich Preller, a good friend from the Altenburg days.

*L*iszt—*incomparable virtuoso, a sometimes popular, sometimes visionary composer—was also a man of immense kindness.* ABOVE: *One of Liszt's last pianos, above which hangs a portrait of the* composer by B. Blockhorst (1869). OPPOSITE: *The dining room at the Hofgärtnerei, where Liszt loved to play whist during the last years of his life.*

Richard
Wagner
1813–1883

The life of Richard Wagner reads like a novel, a narrative rich in picaresque and tragic, scandalous and distressing events, with the Bayreuth period as a triumphant epilogue. Wagner spent his first sixty years, from 1813 to 1872, tracing a peripatetic course through Leipzig, Dresden, Prague, Königsberg, Riga, Paris, Zurich, Munich, and Lucerne, to cite only the principal stops. At one point or another he found himself proscribed for sedition, hounded as a financial deadbeat, or worshipped by an elite coterie of admirers. Wildly acclaimed at times, he was often rebuffed and forever in pursuit of an elusive glory.

By 1864, when Ludwig II of Bavaria invited him to Munich, Wagner was broke, without prospects, and on the brink of suicide. Now, it seemed, the miraculous prince had come, the royal patron who would make it possible for his operas to be produced. At last, the *cris du coeur* the composer once uttered to Elisa Wille had been heard: "The world owes me what I need. Is it therefore not idiotic to demand that I give up the bits of luxury I desire, all the while that I am preparing such delights for thousands of beings?" For his part, the smitten Ludwig could refuse him nothing, but Wagner had arrived with such heavy baggage that it soon aroused the enmity of first the court and then the capital. The impedimenta included tactlessness and an adulterous affair with Cosima, wife and daughter respectively of two trusting friends, the conductor Hans von Bülow and the great pianist Franz Liszt. Then there was Wagner's revolutionary past, the time when he mounted the barricades alongside Bakunin during the Dresden uprising of 1849. Most of all, Munich found the King's court musician extraordinarily expensive to keep, nicknaming him "Lolus," after the notorious Lola Montez, the favorite courtesan of Ludwig II's father. By late 1865 Richard Wagner would again be obliged to renew his wandering.

In April 1866 Wagner settled at Tribschen near Lucerne, together with Cosima, whom he was to marry

four years later. Here their daughter Eva and their son Siegfried were born. The family occupied a beautiful and dignified house on a wooded promontory overlooking a lake colonized by swans. The Tribschen years proved to be the happiest in the composer's life. Free of material concern, thanks to Ludwig's generosity, Wagner set about writing most of *Siegfried, Die*

"*F*inished, the eternal work!
At the top of the mountain,
The city of the gods:
Splendidly resplendent
The brilliant edifice!
How I dreamt it would be,
How my desire made it possible,
Strong and beautiful
It surges up,
Majestic, superb edifice!"
Richard Wagner,
Das Rheingold, *scene 2.*

OPPOSITE: *The tomb of Richard Wagner in the park at Wahnfried, his "ultimate happiness."*
ABOVE: *Lithographic portrait of Richard Wagner after a watercolor by Clementine Stocker-Escher (1853).*

Meistersinger von Nürnberg, Die Götterdämerung, and the *Siegfried Idyll* (originally *Tribschen Idyll*), that ravishing serenade composed as a tribute to Cosima on her thirty-third birthday. Streams of friends visited from all over Europe, especially Paris, among them Judith Gautier, the daughter of Théophile, Villiers de l'Isle-Adam, Catulle Mendès, and the fascinating Augusta Holmes. Another frequent guest in the house was a young admirer named Friedrich Nietzsche, whom Wagner met while living at Tribschen.

*"On the snowy peaks live the gods,
And Valhalla is their domain.
They are creatures of light. . . ."
Richard Wagner,* Siegfried,
act I, scene 2.

OPPOSITE: *"The space meant for a larger stairwell, rising the complete height of the house, and illuminated by a skylight, has now become a great hall."*

Lucerne, however, was not the place where Wagner could realize his grandiose dream, which was to have a theatre specially designed for his *Gesamtkunstwerke.* The epiphany came in April 1871 at Bayreuth, where he announced that "the particular character and the location of this charming town [are] just what I need." Bayreuth, in fact, could boast a cultural past of some brilliance. In the seventeenth and eighteenth centuries, for example, it had been a center of intense musical activity, to such a degree that Margravine Wilhelmine, the sister of Friedrich the Great and a composer in her own right, commissioned a wonderful Baroque opera house.

Ludwig II, alas, did not like Bayreuth, finding it too close to Prussia, which he despised; nonetheless, he paid for the land out of his own pocket. The construction of *Wahnfried,* or "Peace from Illusion," was

assigned to the architect Carl Wölfel, who created a large square house "in the Roman manner." On 18 April 1874, after two years in a rented but comfortable dwelling, Richard, Cosima, and their three children moved into Wahnfried.

Oddly enough, Cosima's voluminous journals, as well as her letters, contain no more than a few brief references to what Wagner called his "ultimate happi-

"Here is the piano, here too my large writing table, with a handsome top made of Bayreuth marble; opposite, Cosima's smaller table—a bit farther, a table laden with gifts and souvenirs.

All about, furniture to accommodate numerous visitors. The whole is illuminated by an apsidal extension which gives on to the garden, and it is here that I work when daily affairs permit. . . ."

ness." Perhaps the imperious Cosima viewed such details as irrelevant, even though she never hesitated to join her considerable staff in the everyday task of housekeeping. It is from Wagner himself that we have the best description of Wahnfried, written in a letter of 1 October 1874 to "My Heaven-sent friend, my lord, and my King full of grace," i.e., Ludwig II. "The space of an ordinary and comfortable house, composed of a raised ground floor and an upper story, has been disposed by me in such a way as to reduce to a minimum height the ceiling of the upper floor where my family live. I have, by contrast, given to the rooms on the lower floor a ceiling of maximum height . . . which affords me a grand room now much admired by my visitors. . . . [This room] contains all my possessions. The wall panels shelter my collection of books; our pictures are hung there; on every side are desks enclosing our papers and our documents. Here is the piano, here too my large writing table, with a handsome top made of Bayreuth marble; opposite, Cosima's smaller table—a bit farther, a table laden with gifts and souvenirs. All about, furniture to accommodate numerous visitors. The whole is illuminated by an apsidal extension which gives on to the garden, and it is here that I work when daily affairs permit. . . . The space meant for a larger staircase, rising the complete height of the house, and illuminated by a skylight, has now become a great hall. . . . The marbles, that is, the six statues by Zumbusch, which my gracious benefactor gave me at an earlier date, preside here as do the busts of my wife and myself."

On the walls of this skylit hall Cosima embedded a series of oil paintings narrating the cycle of four operas making up *Der Ring des Niebelungen*. The six statues mentioned by the composer were also representations of Wagnerian heroes: Lohengrin, Siegfried, Tannhäuser, Tristan, Walter von Stolzing, and Parsifal. It is almost as if the place were not so much the house of Richard Wagner as a temple to the great man.

Put another way, Wahnfried might be described as a kind of presbytery to the true temple, the *Festspielhaus*, from which it is totally inseparable. Although construction began on 22 May 1872, the revolutionary "Festival Theatre" would not witness the first performance of the complete *Ring* until August 1876. Even

this proved too soon for the underwriters, who lost a fortune in the undertaking. The Festspielhaus did not reopen until 1882, for the premiere of *Parsifal*, the only opera Wagner composed at Wahnfried.

Meanwhile, Wagner never ceased traveling, always in search of funds, as well as in satisfaction of an incurable wanderlust. Thus, it was in Venice that he would die, on 13 February 1883, while living in the Palazzo Loredan Vendramin Calergi on the Grand Canal. His remains, returned in triumph to Bayreuth, were buried "in the very shade of Wahnfried," just as he had requested.

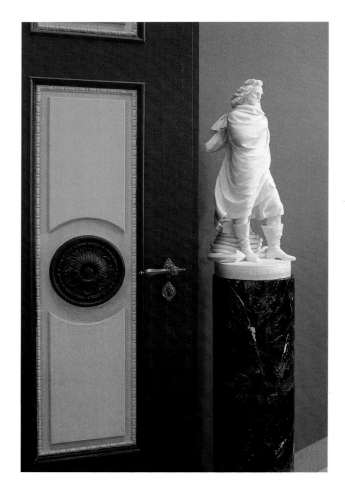

"*The* marbles, that is, the six statues by Zumbusch, which my gracious benefactor gave me at an earlier date, preside here as do the busts of my wife and myself."

"Now greet Valhalla for me, Greet Wotan for me Greet Wälse and all the heroes. . . ."
Richard Wagner, Die Walküre, act II, scene 4.

Giuseppe
Verdi
1813–1901

Verdi, that veteran traveler at the height of the rail-road craze, helped inaugurate the first wagons-lits, as he commuted from opera house to opera house—Milan, Venice, Paris, London, St. Petersburg, Vienna, Berlin—always with a timetable in his frockcoat pocket. Meanwhile, no man was ever more attached his own native soil.

Verdi, quite literally, would remain forever rooted in the countryside around Parma. Born on 10 October 1813 in Le Roncole, he lived first in tiny Busseto, a few miles distant, residing at the beautiful Palazzo Orlandi, which happened to be the home of his patron, a wealthy local merchant named Antonio Barezzi. In 1844, after the works of his "galley years" began generating royalties, Verdi bought a property near Le Roncole, which, in 1848, he exchanged for the Sant' Agata estate on the outskirts of Busseto. He settled there in 1851 and launched into the endless process of refurbishing the house, embellishing the garden, and enlarging the domain.

Verdi, furthermore, never flagged in his devotion to this terrain, despite the Bussetans who had poisoned his youth with their rivalries and who now snubbed his companion, Giuseppina Strepponi. Nor was he put off by the raw climate of the Emilian plain. Sant' Agata would quite simply be the composer's principal residence to the end of his life a half-century later. Playwrights, impresarios, theatre directors, librettists, conductors, divas—all came to work with the master or to pay their respects, especially during summer, when snow, rain, and flood did not make the roads impassable.

In reality, there are several Verdis at Sant' Agata, the most elusive of whom is undoubtedly the author of *Nabucco* and *Rigoletto*, *Aïda* and *Otello*. This is because the man whose music expressed emotions verging on paroxysm was in reality a prudent, reserved, and even secret person. His bedroom, with its polished mahogany furniture and its sober, reassuring

air, betrays nothing of the transports experienced by the composer while alone with his creative work: "When I am one on one with myself, engaged with my notes, my heart beats faster, tears pour from my eyes; my emotion and my joy are beyond measure." Given this confession, it can hardly surprise that Verdi kept his piano only a step away from the bed.

Verdi himself redesigned his room, just as he did the rest of the house. Even more astonishingly, at least for the nineteenth century, he installed his bedroom and that of Giuseppina on the ground floor. In fact, this was the garden floor, where the rooms open directly on to nature, an arrangement reflecting Verdi's love of the bucolic world and the land he owned. In Giuseppina's bedroom, where a second piano attests to her early career as a great opera singer, a special

Son of a poor peasant who could barely pay the rent on his house and the land he farmed, Verdi was determined to become a man of property. OPPOSITE: *Bust of Giuseppina Strepponi by* *Pietro Tenerani (1798–1869).* ABOVE: *Anonymous photographic portrait of Giuseppe Verdi (late nineteenth century).*

place is reserved for paintings memorializing a series of beloved pets: a parrot and the dogs Lùlù and Lorito.

Elsewhere, the disposition and decoration of the house conformed in every respect to the canons of taste then prevailing among the well-off. There is a small parlor, a large parlor, a library, a dining room, and the inevitable billiard room. Billiards, as well as cards, constituted one of Verdi's favorite pastimes, played with a curious mixture of fury and cool calculation. No less important is the kitchen, virtually theatrical in its dimensions and its glittering, even resonating collection of copper pots and pans. Here, in Emilia where cookery rivaled religion, Verdi was a fervent practitioner, indeed a high priest. He gladly

made pasta from scratch and shared his recipes with friends. At St. Petersburg, where he went to conduct the premiere of *La Forza del Destino*, Verdi joined in a competition with the great actress Adelaide Ristori, who too happened to be in the Russian capital. Giuseppina knew how it would turn out: "If La Ristori believes she can beat us, devastate us with her *tagliatelle*, Verdi counts on eclipsing her with his *risotto*, which, in truth, he does divinely."

The reception rooms at Sant' Agata would be perfect as sets for *La Traviata*, complete with velvet curtains, Oriental rugs, paneling, and heavy furniture in the eclectic, ornate style of the period. They are also stuffed with bibelots, *curiosa*, and, most of all, souvenirs from the career of the most universally feted musician of his time. Hidden from the curious and the opportunistic by massed trees and high walls, the master of this bourgeois redoubt made living well the best revenge upon those childhood years in his parents' poor tavern/grocery in Le Roncole. Sant' Agata also made up for all the furnished hotel rooms and flats he had had to endure during his years of constant travel.

For Verdi the garden constituted one of the most important aspects of Sant' Agata. As Giuseppina Strepponi wrote: ". . . we have begun to plant a garden which right away became known as the garden of Peppina. . . . It is now his garden, and I can tell you that he reigns there like a czar, until I am now reduced to a few square feet of soil."

The statues in the garden were made by the Venetian sculptor Giuseppe Berardi, known as Torreti (1682–1743).

But the house was merely one of the three elements that made up Verdi's daily life at Sant' Agata. The second element was the garden. In their early days at the villa, Giuseppina (Peppina) wrote to her friend Clara Maffei as follows: "With the greatest pleasure, we have begun planting a garden, which right away became known as the garden of Peppina. Now fully laid out, it is *his* garden, and I can tell you that he reigns there like a czar, until I am presently reduced to a few square feet of soil."

"*V*erdi is transformed into an architect, and I could not describe all the comings and goings, and the ballet of beds, chests, and furniture during the work on the house. Suffice it to say that, except for the kitchen and the cowshed, there is not one corner in the house where we have not slept." *Giuseppina Strepponi to Countess Clara Maffei (1867).*

Like the term "villa," as the Romans understood it, the word "garden" is rather too modest. The floor-to-ceiling bedroom windows open on to a gravel-covered terrace furnished with classic outdoor furniture and ornamented with flowers in both pots and small beds. In the vast park, with its double rows of poplars and plane trees, the latter running all the way to the fields, the composer allowed nature a generous degree of "managed" liberty. Over the years, Verdi haunted the nurseries in Genoa during his winter stays there, or sent his friends to make the rounds on his behalf. Chief among the delegates was the great conductor Angelo Mariani, the pioneer champion of Wagner in Italy. In that "solitude shot through day and night with a silence which both startles and enchants," as the Orientalist Italo Pizzi described Sant' Agata, visitors moved from surprise to surprise. Among the novelties is a tiny island at the center of a small artificial lake, where, for the want of a better facility, Verdi and Giuseppina took a bath one day. Also a grotto (*Aïda*'s tomb, of course), an ice cave under a hillock, a dovecote, statues from the Villa Pallavicino in Bussetto, and even a chapel. Verdi, although a confirmed anticlerical and agnostic, had this last feature built so that Giuseppina would not have to attend services at the village church

Verdi exaggerated a bit when he wrote to his publisher, Ricordi: "My house is modest; I own no fine furniture, or almost none. When I do buy some the pieces will not be made of either rosewood or mahogany."

farms, always ready to take up pitchfork or shovel. One of the great challenges in Verdi's country life was the protection of his fields from floods whenever the three rivers threatened to overflow. Problems arising from the first chemical fertilizers, or those of a dysfunctional steam pump, worried Verdi far more than the details of an operatic production. Back at home in the evening, exhausted and covered in mud, he holed up in a small room next to his bedroom and spent the evening poring over the next day's accounts: household expenses, garden, seed, crops, livestock, tenants, etc. In the course of his travels, whatever the fatigue or the crises of rehearsal, Verdi never forgot Sant' Agata. There he always returned laden with furniture, objets d'art, and plants, as already noted, but also agrarian innovations discovered at the Universal Exhibitions in Paris, London, and Turin.

A bear with a heart of gold, Verdi was a chronic grumbler, forever inveighing against opera houses, impresarios, publishers, conductors, tenors and sopranos, instrumentalists and choruses, stagehands and even the audience. Nor did he spare Sant' Agata, cursing the huge sums it consumed, the visitors, who were either too numerous or too few, the neighbors, the frosts and gales of winter, the scorching droughts of summer, the "blockhead" domestics, gardeners, and farmers. In every instance, the composer's outbursts were nothing so much as proof of a tough, passionate love.

and there suffer the scorn and whispering of the local bigots.

Finally, beyond the parallel rows of plane trees, between the River Arda, the River Ongina flowing along the edge of the park, and the Po, lay thousands of acres of land, where lived the Verdi whom Verdi preferred: the peasant. Indeed, "peasant," not "land owner," was how the composer styled himself in conversation and correspondence alike. In every kind of weather, on horseback or in a cart, he made the rounds of his

The small bedroom at the hotel in Milan where Verdi died has been carefully reconstructed at Sant' Agata. On one of the chairs rests a cushion embroidered with the Verdi monogram, a cypher which, in the 1880s, also served as a label for the products of the composer's sausage factory.
RIGHT: *Portrait bust of Giuseppe Verdi.*

Johann
Strauss II
1825–1899

Johann Strauss? *The Beautiful Blue Danube?* The Viennese waltz? But which Johann Strauss, the father or the son? To complicate matters further, Vienna's Danube is not the actual river but rather a canalized tributary. Moreover, its muddy waters, flowing well away from the urban center, have never been even slightly blue. As for the waltz, its origins, though obscure, are certainly not Viennese. Evidently the three-quarter fad began in Berlin, a random fact that scarcely bothered nineteenth-century Vienna. Its citizens were much too caught up in the giddy pleasure of dancing the night away under the great chandeliers of ballrooms named Sperl, Mondschein, Tivoli, Dianabad, and Odeon.

The first Johann, born in 1804, was the son of one Franz Strauss, who ran a cabaret called "The Good Shepherd" *(Zum guten Hirten)* but ended up drowning himself in—what else?—the Danube. His grandfather, Michael Strauss, was a "converted Jew," according to the marriage rolls at St. Stephen's Cathedral. This little detail presented a problem for the Nazis, who were reluctant to proscribe the Strausses as they had the "vulgar" Mendelssohn and Mahler. Finally, they circumvented the problem by removing the telltale page and replacing it with a skillfully calligraphed forgery.

In 1815 the waltz swept through every important salon in the Austrian capital, thanks to the Congress of Vienna and its many diplomats from all over Europe. Then, in 1819, came Weber's *Invitation to the Dance,* whose success endowed the waltz with something like a musical patent of nobility. A prudish minority, needless to say, did not succumb so easily, among them England's Dr. Burney, who thought it scandalous that hands could now venture, in public, where they had never before been. But in Vienna, whose citizens could not resist the urge to dance, the waltz craze verged on madness. Johann Strauss I, together with his friend Josef Lanner, caught the trend and ran with it, initially at the "Red Cockerel" *(Rorer Hahn),* where both their

orchestra and their compositions were all the rage at Carnival time.

The year 1825 proved eventful for Johann Strauss. He married the boss's pregnant daughter, who shortly thereafter, on 25 October, gave birth to Johann II. This was at Rofranogasse 76, but the house, like most of the Strauss sites, has long since been pulled down. During the same period, Johann I broke with Josef Lanner, who promptly celebrated the event by introducing the *Separation Waltz.* For the next six years Strauss worked at the Sperl, the largest and most elegant ballroom in Vienna. He would now manage a company of 200 musicians and virtually monopolize the ballroom scene in Vienna. Everyone who heard Johann Strauss I confirmed his talent, as did Hector Berlioz: "He . . . has written such ravishing things for his dance orchestra that they would be welcome in many operas."

Like the house where Johann Strauss II was born, most of the family's dwelling places in Vienna have been demolished. Only the house occupied by Johann II has survived, at Praterstrasse 54. Now a museum, it was abandoned by the "Waltz King" in 1875 for a splendid villa in Hietzing. Three years later Strauss had a veritable palace (a palais in Viennese parlance) erected on the Igelgasse. OPPOSITE: *The stairwell in the Praterstrasse house.* ABOVE: *Portrait of Johann Strauss II by A. Eisenmenger.*

As for Johann Strauss II, it soon became clear that he would be as good a musician as his father but with a special gift for the violin. Johann I, unfortunately, longed to see his son in a more "respectable" career, perhaps that of a notary, a banker, or a military officer. Disaster was avoided after Johann I abandoned his wife and children for life with a mistress, thereby liberating Johann II to live as he wished. In 1844, the nineteen-year-old musician assembled his own orchestra and became an immediate success at Franz Dommayer's beautiful venue near Schönbunn.

This triggered a blood feud in the Strauss family, with Johann I pitted against Johann II. The elder Strauss even stipulated exclusivity in his contracts so as to lock his younger rival out of every ballroom in Vienna. Still, Johann II, though frequently obliged to tour, sometimes managed to eclipse his father in critical favor. During the 1848 revolution, Johann I sided with established order, for whose cause he wrote the *Radetzky March*, while Johann II supported the liberals, confirming his commitment in the *Freedom March*. The "War of the Strausses" came to a brutal end in 1849,

"*S*trauss inhabits a musical universe whose doors were opened to us by Beethoven and Weber—a marvelous universe of rhythm, an infinitely fertile field where those who cultivate it will reap beautiful harvests." Hector Berlioz.

when Johann I perished of scarlet fever, leaving his talented son to become the undisputed "Waltz King" of Vienna.

Johann II reigned at the Tenne, with its little railway and Turkish harem; in the English gardens at the Neue Welt; in the Odeon ballrooms, so vast that each resembled a desert when empty of dancers; at the Sofienbad, which, in 1863, was revamped to look like the Piazza San Marco in Venice, complete with gondolas. He also held forth at the "poor folks' balls,"

Johann Strauss II composed nothing for the organ, even though the instrument, reduced to a size suitable for parlors, was often an essential feature in the great bourgeois houses of the mid-nineteenth century.

for which the wealthy came disguised as tramps, as well as at the Dianabad, where, in 1867, Strauss gave the first performance of his Opus 314: *An der Schönen blauen Donau,* otherwise known as *The Beautiful Blue Danube* or simply the *Blue Danube Waltz.*

Johann II lived at Praterstrasse 54, a handsome house that he quitted in 1875 for a splendid villa in Hietzing, before moving in 1878 to Igelgasse 4, where he had built a *palais,* as the Viennese call their mansions. Today only the Praterstrasse residence survives, transformed into a museum. Nothing is known of what it was like in Strauss's time, although Biedermeier undoubtedly remained the established style (see pages 25–26). As for the Igelstrasse *palais,* several pieces of furniture, notably an apartment organ and a music stand, suggest that it was decorated in the Germanic Neo-Rococo manner, later known as the *Historismus* or "historical" or "revivalist" style. This is confirmed by Franz von Bayros's picture entitled *A Soirée at the Home of Johann Strauss,* a work of 1894. Here the curtains are heavy, the carpets thick, and the overall design complicated, including wall panels painted and gilded à la Louis XV and furniture dominated by cabriole legs and cursive lines. Everything is sumptuous, even ostentatious, and a bit stuffy.

In the year 1867, when Austria was militarily and politically defeated by Prussia, driven from Italy, and generally coming apart at its Imperial seams, the lilting frivolity of the *Blue Danube Waltz, An Artist's Life (Künstlerleben),* and *Vienna Blood (Wiener Blut)* made the Viennese forget their setbacks. "A desperate situation, but not serious" was the mantra heard in Vienna's salons. Everything was in a mad, waltz-like whirl, what with the telegrams, the patriots, the students, the bandits, the Vienna Woods, the lawsuits, the charitable ladies, the demolition of the ancient ramparts, etc. Johann II's catalogue, listing thousands of waltzes, polkas, quadrilles, and marches, is one of the most eclectic in the history of music.

Viennese kitsch attained what was undoubtedly its zenith in 1872, in Boston no less. Invited to the United States, Johann II, aided by 100 assistant conductors, led an ensemble of 10,000 musicians and a chorus of 20,000 before an audience numbering 100,000 people. Besieged by Boston ladies demanding a lock of hair, the Waltz King had his valet distribute clippings from his black Newfoundland!

In the early 1870s, Johann II took on a genre that was new to him, the operetta. This time the reception was somewhat muted, despite the success of *The Bat* (*Die Fledermaus;* 1874) and *The Gypsy Baron* (*Der Zigeunerbaron;* 1885). Still, like his father, he was respected, even admired by the greatest musicians of his time. Richard Wagner placed Strauss's waltzes among "the original and most lovable phenomena in all of public art"; moreover, they exceeded "in grace, refinement, and true musical content most of the fabricated products imported from abroad." Johannes Brahms went even further, declaring that "of all our colleagues, Strauss is one of my favorites, if not the one I prefer the most." A photograph of 1894 shows Johann II on a terrace at Bad Ischl, where he spent the summer months at Villa Erdödy. Dressed to the nines, his hair and moustache impeccably trimmed, Strauss appears astonishingly youthful next to Brahams, who, with his hermit's beard and rumpled clothes, would scarcely be taken for a man eight years younger than his companion.

At a banquet in 1890 Johann II had declared: "It is from the sun of Vienna that I draw all my strength, from its air on which floats every sound my ear detects, which my heart gathers and my hand notates. . . ." During that same year an opinion poll—already!— had cited him, along with Queen Victoria and Chancellor Bismarck, as one of the three most famous persons in the world. Furthermore, the news of his death, on 3 June 1899, at his Igelgasse *palais,* set off a vast outpouring of emotion. His coffin was borne throughout Vienna, followed by a throng of 100,000 mourners, who continued all the way to his final resting place, next to Brahms opposite Beethoven and Schubert.

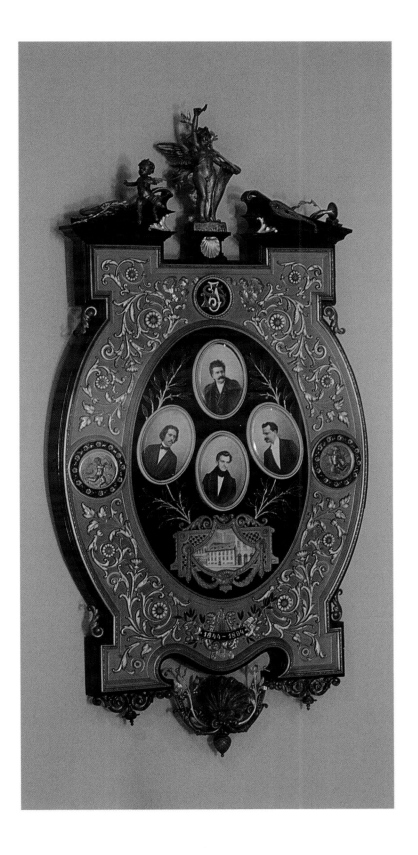

ABOVE: *The Strauss dynasty: Johann Strauss I, Johann Strauss II, and the latter's sons, Josef and Edvard. Today it would be possible to add, among* others, Johann Strauss III (1866–1939), Edvard's son, and Edvard Strauss II (1910–1969), a nephew of Johann II.

Johannes
Brahms
1833–1897

"Here I've found a marvelous and incredibly cheap lodging, so that now I can enjoy the magnificent panorama unhindered. . . . The house stands on the upper reaches of the Caecilienberg. From my rooms I can see mountains on three sides, all covered with flowers, crisscrossing paths, and here and there a few charming little houses." This is how Brahms, writing in May 1865, described the small flat he had just rented at Baden-Baden in what thereafter would be known as "the beautiful house on the hill."

Brahms already knew the Black Forest spa, having spent several days there in 1863, lodged in the home of a surgeon, Dr. Hammer. At the end of July 1864, he stayed with the great Russian pianist/composer Anton Rubinstein but then moved into the Bear Hotel (*Zum Bären*). Here Brahms remained until 10 October, composing, among other pieces, his Piano Quintet in F minor. What held him was in large part the presence of the great pianist Clara Schumann, then living in Baden-Baden between concert tours.

Robert and Clara Schumann had first come into the life of Johannes Brahms on 30 September 1853, a date the younger composer would always endow with an importance equal to that of his own birth (7 May 1833). For him, Robert Schumann represented the artistic ideal at its most uncompromising and lofty. As for Schumann, he confessed to his diary that evening in 1853: "Visit from Brahms. What genius!" Right away Brahms entered the circle of Schumann's most intimate friends, where he would remain after Schumann died on 29 July 1856, always a trusted presence at the side of the widowed Clara. In truth, Brahms's regard for the celebrated pianist—and composer of considerable talent—grew more reverent with each passing year. She, in turn, evinced deep affection for Brahms, despite his being fourteen years her junior.

*I*n Baden-Baden, Brahms rose at daybreak, after which he walked until nine o'clock. He then settled down to work until five o'clock, stopping only for lunch. Following a visit with Clara Schumann, he would resume work, only to return to Clara for dinner, often with friends passing through.
ABOVE: *Johannes Brahms, in a photographic portrait made the day of his arrival in Vienna in 1862.*

The Beautiful House on the Hill

"Here I am! Installed two steps from the Prater, and I can now drink my wine where Beethoven drank his."

Very soon, events would prove Brahms right about Vienna, from which base he won international fame, so that by the time of his Baden-Baden days he was enjoying the first full flower of a brilliant career. At Baden-Baden some 50,000 foreigners came every year to take the waters and try their luck at the casino. Around the rather absurd neo-Corinthian pavilions swarmed a rarefied throng of crowned or uncrowned heads, pedigreed aristocrats and adventurers, flamboyant speculators and fashionable artists. For their pleasure, three concerts were given every day. At Baden-Baden, Brahms met Pauline Viardot, the sister of Maria Malibran and an esteemed singer in her own right. Viardot had just had a veritable palace built near the springs. With her there, as usual, was the great Russian writer Ivan Turgenev. In addition to a fabulous collection of paintings and the original manuscript of *Don Giovanni,* the Viardot mansion boasted a concert hall equipped with an organ built by Cavaillé-Coll, the greatest organ-maker of his day.

Brahms's dwelling, modest in both origin and style, bore no resemblance to that of La Viardot. The composer occupied two small rooms at the top of an unpretentious though delightful house in Lichtental just outside Baden-Baden. The property belonged to Frau Becker, the window of a lawyer. In one of his rooms—known as the "Blue Parlor" for the color of its tiles and fabric-covered walls—Brahms created a study, complete with piano. In the other room—a narrow, simple space in the mansard attic—he installed his narrow bachelor's bed. Of course, he spent considerable time at the home of Clara Schumann, who lived not far away, but even in Vienna his flat was scarcely less spartan than those two rooms in Baden-Baden. Florence May, a young English pianist who worked with Brahms in 1871, left a description of the composer's daily life in Baden-Baden, along with an acutely observed and convincing portrait of the master.

"In Brahms' demeanor there was a mixture of sociability and reserve which gave me the impression of his being a kindly-natured man, but one whom it would be difficult really to know. . . . His manner was absolutely simple and unaffected. . . . I met him [at

Yet, close as their relationship was, it appears never to have evolved beyond the purely platonic.

By the time he appeared in Baden-Baden, Brahms had decided to abandon his native Hamburg for life in Vienna, deeming the Imperial capital the only place where his talent and glory could be fully realized.

"*H*ere I've found a marvelous and incredibly cheap lodging, so that now I can enjoy the magnificent panorama unhindered. . . . The house stands on the upper reaches of the Caecilienberg. From my rooms I can see mountains on three sides, all covered with flowers, crisscrossing paths, and here and there a few ravishing little houses."

Frau Schumann's] continually at the hour of afternoon coffee. . . . and very often, when the coffee-cups were done with, it was my good fortune to listen to the two great artists playing duets; Brahms, the favoured, being always allowed to retain the beloved cigar or cigarette between his lips during the performances. . . . He was a great walker, and had a passionate love of nature. It was his habit during the spring and summer to rise at four or five o'clock and, after making himself a cup of coffee, to go into the woods to enjoy the delicious freshness of the early morning and to listen to the singing of the birds. In adverse weather he could still find something to admire and enjoy."

Brahms appeared rarely at the home of Pauline Viardot, the queen of Baden-Baden. Mme Viardot, after all, belonged to the enemy camp, made up of those who supported Liszt and Wagner in the war declared by "Brahmsians" against the so-called "music of the future" and its various pretensions. Throughout his oeuvre Brahms remained the dedicated classicist, even as he laced his massive, architectonic symphonies and concertos, as well as his polished and refined chamber

*T*he simplicity of the mansarded room at Lichtental is quite in keeping with the composer's taste. Brahms, according to a friend, could sleep almost any-where, on the ground or under a grand piano.

works, with novel thematic developments. From 1865 to 1872 the composer visited Baden-Baden almost every year, staying usually from May through October. The sojourns became part of his self-imposed program, which consisted of concertizing in the winter and composing in the summer. Though an ideal arrangement, it did not always work out; still, while in Baden-Baden, Brahms undertook or completed several of his key masterpieces, including *A German Requiem* (1857–1868) and the Cello Sonata in E flat (1866), the *Liebesliederwalzer* and the *Alto Rhapsody* (1869), and the *Lieder und Gesänge* (1871). In 1873 Clara Schumann sold her house, after which Brahms spent less time in the spa city. Yet it was here, in 1876, that he completed his First

Symphony and, the following year, his Second Symphony, sometimes called the *Lichtentaler.*

Beginning in 1879, Brahms gave up Baden-Baden in favor of Austria's Bad Ischl, the spa preferred by the Imperial family. He also began his custom of making lengthy forays into Italy and Sicily. Baden-Baden, however, continued to claim a special place in the composer's heart. On 13 September 1883 he gave a birthday party for Clara Schumann at the Hotel Zum Bären. It was also in Baden-Baden that, in 1887, he joined Clara Schumann and a pair of great string players—cellist Robert Hausmann and violinist Joseph Joachim—for a run-through of the Double Concerto. Following two days of further work, the new composition received its

premiere on 23 September before an invited audience in the Louis xv Hall at the Kurzhaus. On 8 May 1896 Brahms wrote to Clara Schumann: "I've learned that you are to be in Baden-Baden. Please let me know when and for how long. I've always had a particular fondness for Baden-Baden, and I would love to take this opportunity to see the landscape again—as well as the friend I've loved for such a long time."

Brahms never again saw either Baden-Baden or Clara Schumann. The latter died on 20 May, a few days after Brahms wrote his note, and he would not long survive her. On 3 April 1897 the great composer breathed his last in the flat he had occupied in Vienna since 1871, at Karlgasse 4.

The "Blue Parlor." The modest character of the lodging should not be taken to suggest that Brahms's career was difficult. According to one of his friends:

"He is so universally appreciated that he could become rich solely by reason of his compositions, if he wished. Fortunately, that is not the case."

Jules
Massenet
1842–1912

"I had fled the excruciating cold of winter," wrote Massenet in Chapter 23 of his *Souvenirs*. "Spring had arrived, and I was going to rediscover nature at my old Égreville house, ever my consolation, in all its solitary quietude." The composer then added, prior to discussing his progress on *Le Jongleur de Notre-Dame* in 1901: "Indeed, the character of my house, a vestige of the Middle Ages, the whole ambiance in which I found myself at Égreville, would envelop my work in the atmosphere I was re-imagining." From this, one might well conclude that Massenet had retired to some family manor or, at least, to a domain he had owned for a very long time. In fact, he had acquired the Égreville estate only in February of that year, when he was already in his fifty-ninth year.

The son of a blacksmith, Jules Massenet was born on 12 May 1842 at Saint-Étienne south of Lyons. Given the senior Massenet's trade, it is difficult to visualize the family living in the kind of pretentious opulence described by Georges Ohnet in his famous novel. But there is no disputing the fact that by the age of eleven Jules was deemed ready for admission to the Paris Conservatoire. While a student there he often supplemented his meager income by playing in the percussion section of theatre and dance-hall orchestras. In 1859 he won two First Prizes, one for counterpoint and the other for fugue, following them in 1862 with a First Prize for piano. The next year he took the biggest prize of all, the Premier Grand Prix de Rome, which in those days virtually assured the future of a new French composer.

While at the Villa Medici, Massenet had the chance to meet Franz Liszt, an encounter that would have important consequences, albeit personal rather than musical. Liszt introduced Massenet to a young woman, Louise-Constance de Gressy, or more familiarly Ninon, who wished to take piano lessons. Almost immediately the teacher fell in love with his pupil, whom he would indeed marry on 8 October 1866. The

ceremony took place at Avon near Fontainebleau, where the composer's mother-in-law owned a house in which the couple would frequently stay. This was only a few miles from Égreville, and so, while merely a châtelain of recent date, Massenet had for years known this part of the Seine-et-Marne district.

Jules Massenet had his first professional success not in opera but rather in an oratorio, *Marie-Magdeleine*, presented in 1873, with Pauline Viardot among the soloists. In 1877 *Le Roi de Lahore* brought him his first operatic hit, and it would be followed by many others. In 1878 Massenet, at the age of thirty-six, was appointed full professor at the Conservatoire and elected to that most elite of French institutions, the Institut de France. Now, in rapid succession, came the sensational premieres of *Hérodiade* (1881), *Manon* (1884), *Le Cid* (1885), *Esclarmonde* (1889), *Werther* (1892), and *Thaïs* (1894).

*T*he oeuvre of Jules Massenet is enormous. It includes some thirty lyric dramas, sacred as well as profane, and much else that has yet to be explored.
OPPOSITE: *Massenet's bedroom and place of work. The mobile* calendar bears the date on which the composer left Égreville for the last time, on 9 August 1912, four days before his death.
ABOVE: *Photographic portrait of Jules Massenet by H. Manuel.*

The Châtelain of Égreville

The last, one of his most popular operas, was composed, like *Manon* and *Esclarmonde,* for the American soprano Sibyl Sanderson. Later works include *La Navarraise* (1894–1895) and *Sapho* (1897). Along with this abundant production emerged a variety of works in other musical genres—religious dramas, symphonic pieces, songs, and works for the piano. While the critics sometimes had reservations about a composer they regarded as "conservative," Claude Debussy, an ardent supporter of Massenet, explained in *Monsieur Croche antidilettante* that "his confreres had difficulty forgiving that ability to please which is precisely his gift."

Massenet divided his time between an apartment in Paris and village sojourns on the coast of Normandy or at Pont-de-l'Arche on the Seine near Rouen. After three decades of intense activity, he sought a house close enough to Paris for easy travel and yet far enough to escape opportunistic visitors. The latter, given the transportation available at the time, could not travel round-trip from Paris in a single day, and very likely Égreville did not offer much in the way of hotels. Before long, however, progress would overtake the retiring composer, who, in 1905, waxed indignant in Homeric rhetoric to write of how, "thundering at sixty to the hour," rather like "Jupiter thundering in the sky," the automobile of his friend Pedro Gailhard, director of the Paris Opéra, erupted into the courtyard of the "old house."

Old it certainly was, with traces of a château on the site since at least the mid-twelfth century. In 1540 the Duchesse d'Étampes, a favorite of François I, had the present structure erected, retaining from the old

"It is raining, the sky is overcast. Excellent for the trees, but not so good for my tomatoes. Yesterday, we made 15 livres of pear jam (successfully). Is that enough?"

"La casa," "the solitude of the summers"—such were the nicknames Massenet gave to his "old house."

ing, the sky is overcast. Excellent for the trees, but not so good for my tomatoes. Yesterday, we made 15 *livres* of pear jam (successfully). Is that enough? Yes? The apples are in mad profusion. The garden is all soft green and red. . . ."

Massenet, however, was not in Égreville to retire. One has only to consider the contents of his upstairs bedroom, with its "large work table—a famous table, I'm proud to say, since it once belonged to the illustrious Diderot"—its mute keyboard, and an extraordinary Pleyel equipped with four side drawers designed

castle a single round tower, vestiges of which survive to this day. Her niece laid out the gardens and had the deep moats excavated, only to leave them entirely dry. During the Restoration period (1815–1830), Égreville fell into the hands of the notorious demolition team known as the "Black Band." One of its worst vandals pulled down the central gallery as well as the tower for whatever price the raw materials would fetch. The tower still contained a salon decorated with sixteenth-century frescoes and sculpture.

Égreville, notwithstanding, remains an irresistibly charming château. Massenet took infinite care of the gardens and fields, as well as the surrounding woods that separated the house from the marshy plain. Gradually, he rounded out the little domain until, ten years after its acquisition, the estate had grown to 250 acres of land. Worried about the snakes infesting the grassy moats, Massenet wrote to his son-in-law Léon Bessand: "Please arrange for the dispatch to Égreville (with all due precaution) 6 hedgehogs at 2.50 to 3 francs a piece. . . ." Save for the hedgehogs, the manor did not lack for animals, given the presence of the dog Dudu, nicknamed "the postman's terror," the cat Zouzou, a rabbit appropriated from the composer's grandson, and the ass Coco. A true "gentleman farmer," Massenet reveled in the pleasures of country life: "It is rain-

"*T*he house is divine in the autumn. Excellent fireplace and delicious weather outside." Massenet correspondence, 1890. OPPOSITE AND OVERLEAF: *The large parlor at the Château d'Égreville.*

TOP: *At the foot of the stairs a poster announcing the premiere of* Manon. ABOVE: *On the mantelpiece a bronze portrait bust of the composer by the sculptor Ringel d'Illsach.*

to hold papers and scores. This last emerged from an era when industry also produced a "billiard piano," a "piano convertible into a bed, a desk, etc.," and even a piano furnished with a detachable foot warmer!

A piano? But in his *Souvenirs* did he not write—or have it written—as follows: "Never owning a piano at home, especially at Égreville. . . ."? Is this plausible, for a composer who frequently worked out his harmonies on the keyboard? In fact, the prudent Massenet bruited this fiction about in the hope of discouraging singers who might otherwise have camped outside his door in the hope of auditioning for the master. Despite his denials, Massenet even kept a second piano in the main parlor at Égreville.

The furniture that survived the successive military occupations of World War II is comfortable and traditional, offering luxury without ostentation. Particularly notable among the numerous mementos, all carefully arranged in a small vitrine, are the rather stiff photographs from the composer's halcyon days at the Villa Medici and the slender drumsticks with which the young Massenet supplemented his small income.

In addition to *Le Jongleur de Notre-Dame*, Massenet worked on *Chérubin* and *Cléopatre* at Égreville, as well as on a piano concerto he had commenced forty years earlier at the Villa Medici. Beginning in 1902, he went almost every year for the season at Monte Carlo. Here, in that other opera house designed by Charles Garnier (the architect of the Paris Opéra), Raoul Gunsbourg revived Massenet's theatrical works and gave the premieres of still others, including *Thérèse* and *Don Quichotte*. In 1906 the revival of *Le Roi de Lahore* was especially memorable, for the sensational performance given by a dancer named Mata Hari.

While in the principality Massenet rejoiced in the "clear and good sun of the Midi" and "that sea which, from the Côte d'Azur and the Riviera, along the lacy coast of Italy, unrolls its transparent waves all the way to ancient Hellas. . . ." In Monte Carlo he also took pleasure in being the focus of an attentive as well as glittering society. Because Louise Massenet spent much of her time at various spas, her husband rather too often found himself alone during long days and evenings at Égreville. And if one may judge from the meal offered to Pedro Gailhard during his automobile stop

at the château—"sardines as hors d'oeuvre, cheese for dessert"—the gourmandise evoked in *Souvenirs* must have known only rare satisfaction.

Massenet's health had been deteriorating for several years when, on 9 August 1912, it suddenly grew much worse, prompting him to leave for Paris and consultations with his doctors. He died in the capital on 13 August. Shortly before, the composer, or his ghost writer, had added to *Souvenirs* a series of "posthumous thoughts" in which he expanded upon his last home, Égreville: "Oh, the beautiful cemetery! In the midst of fields, its silence perfect for those who reside there. . . ." The narrator then has Massenet's Paris concierge, in the Rue de Vaugirard, respond to all future visitors: "Alas! Monsieur has departed without leaving us an address."

*T*he Château d'Égreville is one of the rare *lieux de mémoirs* in France dedicated to composers. In addition to Massenet's furniture and *objets d'art*, the old manor house contains a collection of posters, all together making a rich pictorial history of his operatic career. ABOVE: A miniature of Sibyl Sanderson, the American soprano who created the title roles in Manon and Thaïs, shown along with Massenet's watch and wallet.

Edvard
Grieg
1843–1907

Nina and Edvard Grieg did not have a house of their own until 1885, eighteen years after they had married. The dwelling, built to order, was called *Troldhaugen,* meaning "Troll Hill." Until that moment, Grieg's international career, as composer, virtuoso pianist, and conductor, had repeatedly forced the couple to put off their plans for a permanent home.

Edvard Grieg was born in Bergen on 15 June 1843 into a family who made music a central part of their lives. His mother, a piano teacher, had developed a wide following, while on his father's side there had been several amateur members of the Bergen Orchestra. Yet, it was only after the great violinist Ole Bull intervened that the senior Griegs allowed their son to enroll at the Hochschule in Leipzig, the famous conservatory founded by Mendelssohn and the school of choice for most Scandinavian music students. Once there, Grieg suffered terrible bouts of homesickness, but steadfastly persevered. Finally, he would acquire the solid theoretical foundation and the commitment essential to the development of a musical language distinctively national or Norwegian.

Back in Bergen, Grieg made a successful concert debut in 1862 and began the process of forging

his own style and personality, the fruits of which are *Melodies of the Heart,* based on poems by Hans Christian Andersen, and the *Humoresques* for piano. Meanwhile, he became romantically involved with his first cousin, Nina Hagerup, an excellent pianist in her own right as well as a soprano of great talent. This unsettled the young woman's mother, a rather well-known actress, who, despite or because of the close family ties and her career in the theatre, took a dim view of a marriage between her daughter and a twenty-year-old pianist in whom she had no confidence. "He is nothing, he knows nothing, and he writes music no one wants to hear," she declared. The two young people, although secretly engaged in 1864, would not marry until 1867, after Nina had come of age. Still, the bride's parents refused to attend the wedding. Later, in an ironic twist of fate, they ended up financially dependent upon their son-in-law.

"A bristling, indomitable, fiery mane reinforces the profile, endowing the physiognomy with an almost disconcerting heroism, and the green eyes, in which the shifting color of waves appears to slumber, allow us to plunge to dark depths where poetry sleeps. . . ." *Maurice Bigeon,* Les Révoltés scandinaves *(1894).* ABOVE: *Edvard Grieg, by an anonymous photographer.*

Nina Grieg was not only wife and muse but also an incomparable interpreter of her husband's music. During their tours all over Europe, they were often billed together. Steadily, year by year the Norwegian

He walked here by my side,
This great musical poet;
I listened to the flowing waters,
Their cadence the softest
  imaginable,
And never again in this world,

However often I trod this path,
Have I entirely grasped how
  precious
Nature was to me in that
  place.
Bjørnstjerne Bjørnson (1899).

composer rose to musical eminence, thanks especially to the famous Piano Concerto in A minor (1868) and the music for Bjørnstjerne Bjørnson's *Sigurd* and Henrik Ibsen's *Peer Gynt*, both of the playwrights Grieg's friends. In Rome, Grieg won the admiration of Franz Liszt, who, in 1870, played the great concerto from the manuscript—at sight!

Tchaikovsky, who met the Griegs during their early days at Troldhaugen, has left us a marvelous word portrait of the couple: "I saw come into the room a middle-aged man, quite short and extremely fragile in

blance of Edvard and Nina Grieg, who were, after all, very closely related in their blood lines.

For the site of their house, the Griegs chose a promontory overlooking Nordåsvannet, near the village of Hop, a dozen kilometers from Bergen. It had every advantage: reasonable cost, unbroken quietude, despite the proximity of Norway's largest city, a magnificent view, and, also, the nearby presence of an intimate friend, Frants Beyer. Beyer lived in Naesset on the opposite side of the lake, requiring only a few oar strokes for the friends to pay one another frequent visits. On 24 April 1885 Nina and Edvard Grieg moved into their new home.

The villa, designed by Schak Bull, another cousin as well as an architect, is a sober and well-balanced structure. Actually, the glazed veranda, providing entrance to the villa, was built in a Victorian gingerbread style but then simplified at a later date. Standing tall above the cream-colored dwelling is a sort of square tower crowned with a terrace offering a splendid view over the gardens, the lake, and the hills.

The interior boasts walls of unfinished wood, in keeping with Norwegian tradition. The golden hue of the pine harmonizes with the darker gold of the doors and furniture, as well as with the lighter shade of the floors. The house comprises only two stories, the upper one divided into bedrooms and the lower into the parlor, the dining room, and what was once the kitchen. This is now host to memorabilia, including the composer's trunk, its scuffed leather a witness to frequent travel. The kitchen, in any event, was never a place favored by Nina, who freely admitted her culinary incapacity and did not hesitate to offer her guests cold meals. Rarely did she venture beyond pastry, and in the event of the latter she took care to seal off the kitchen so as not to be disturbed in what she deemed a venture fraught with peril.

The dining room and parlor are simply furnished in a comfortable, tasteful manner. Inevitably one's attention is drawn to the handsome concert Steinway in the parlor, a gift to the Griegs in 1892 from the music lovers of Bergen in honor of the couple's silver wedding anniversary. A second gift, on the same occasion, is Werenskiold's painting entitled *Playing Children,* which now hangs in the dining room. The large

appearance, one shoulder higher than the other, his blond hair combed back, a thin, almost boyish beard and mustache. He has uncommon charm, blue eyes, not very large but strangely fascinating, like the look of a beguiling child and full of candor. . . . As for Mme Grieg, I must say right off that she was as sympathetic, pleasant, simple, and unaffected as her celebrated husband." The Russian composer's striking description is amply supported by all manner of pictorial imagery, as is the fact of the almost twin-like resem-

Danish landscape over the piano, framed in gold and ebony, the chandelier in the parlor, and the magnificent silver surtout in the dining room—all gifts marking Grieg's sixtieth birthday in 1903—attest to the affection in which the composer was universally held.

It should be noted that Troldhaugen does not contain a workroom or studio. This was set up outside, among the trees, near the lake shore, in a cabin the composer described as "my little atelier in which I place all my hopes." The "chalet" has a single, pine-clad room, which Grieg furnished with an upright piano and a small table facing the lake. On the wall hangs a Hardanger fiddle, the kind of traditional violin on which the country musicians played their peasant dances, those *slåtter* which inspired many a Norwegian composer, including Ole Bull. The master's coat and hat still hang on a peg.

It was in the cabin in the woods that Grieg composed many of his *Lyric Pieces* for piano, also the *Haug-tussa* song cycle based on the poems of Arne Garborg. Other works, however, such as the Violin Sonata No. 3 in C minor, the *Symphonic Dances,* and the *Four Psalms* were written in the warmer atmosphere of the "great" house. Actually, the humidity in the cabin frequently made it difficult to work there. Moreover, the climate of Troldhaugen did not at all agree with Grieg, who since childhood had suffered respiratory problems. He was often tempted to sell the house and move to Kristiana (Oslo). "Ah! Troldhaugen," he wrote in his journal, "my weakness for this western country costs me dearly. It will kill me. Yet it is [Troldhaugen] which has given me life, which is the source of my enthusiasm. It is [Troldhaugen] which must live again in my music. . . . I have to make up my mind, to break free of Troldhaugen in order to live in the dry climate I need. However, I cannot resolve the issue. . . ."

Beginning in 1900, Grieg's health took a grave turn for the worse, which did not in any way impede his ongoing activities. From Troldhaugen, in 1907, he wrote to a friend: "Life is short! Before long you will not see me further. And so be it. Life has been good to me and more than I deserved. . . ." On 1 September his doctor and Frants Beyer insisted that he leave the villa and have himself admitted to the hospital in Bergen.

He died there on 4 September, peacefully, just as he had lived. Nina would survive him by twenty-eight years. The couple's ashes repose in a burial vault excavated in the granite of Troldhaugen. Etched on the stone sealing their tomb is a simple epitaph consisting merely of "Edvard/Nina Grieg" lettered out in neo-runic characters.

One of the characteristics common to virtually all Nordic composers is the facility with which their feeling for nature is translated into their works without these becoming descriptive.

PAGES 112–113 AND OPPOSITE: *The large parlor of the Toldhaugen villa.*
ABOVE: *The cabin in the woods where the composer had his studio. It was here, in 1911, that Carl Nielsen, while visiting Troldhaugen, wrote his Violin Concerto.*

Vincent
d'Indy
1851–1931

In 1589 Isaïe d'Indy, a captain in the service of King Henri IV, settled at Boffres in the Vivarais. There he built Chabret, the manor house his descendants still owned in the mid-nineteenth century. During summer holidays it became the gathering place for all manner of cousins, among them, beginning in 1864, the young Vincent d'Indy, on whom the beauty of the Ardèche would make an indelible impression. In 1871, on the threshold of his career, Vincent wrote: "I love, I adore Chabret where I spent the happiest days of my youth. . . . If ever in my musical vocation there may survive some spark of inspiration, if ever I succeed in finding my way and show some talent, I shall owe it all to Chabret, because it was here that first feelings began to emerge, here that for the first time I tasted the beautiful and glimpsed the ideal."

Vincent d'Indy was born in Paris on 27 March 1851. His mother having died during childbirth, the infant boy grew up in the care of his grandmother, Countess Rézia d'Indy. The great lady adored her grandson, but with a tough love, couched in severe principles and driven by an authoritarian temperament, as Vincent would later affirm: "Some children are badly raised. As for myself, I was raised, and there was nothing funny about it, on many a day." The d'Indy family, however, evinced a great love of music. Rézia d'Indy was an excellent pianist, and in 1842 she had the good judgment to help underwrite the first trios of a young César Franck. Her son Wilfrid, Vincent's uncle, was an amateur composer. Vincent studied piano, music, and composition, doing so privately with Marmontel, Diémer, and Lavignac. Thanks to his financial independence, he could have his choice among three vocations: the military, traditional in the d'Indy family; painting and drawing, for which he had considerable talent; and music, which, in the end, would easily claim him. D'Indy also wrote with a fine pen, as we know from his numerous books and newspaper articles, his

voluminous correspondence, the texts of his own operas, and the verses for his songs, which he often published himself.

Vincent d'Indy fought heroically during the siege of Paris (1870). In between the two gunshot wounds he suffered, the composer wrote a scherzo and a volume of memoirs about the Franco-Prussian War. He then became a founding member of the famous SNM (Société Nationale de Musique), an organization dedicated—with success—to the renewal of *ars gallica*. In a surge of optimism, d'Indy submitted his first quartet to César Franck, who very kindly informed the young composer that he still had much to learn. From 1872 to 1876, d'Indy took Franck's courses at the Conservatoire, becoming almost religious in his devotion to the master, like other members of the so-called

Vincent d'Indy, though a militant in music as well as in politics, had a personality far more nuanced than his dogmatic attitudes suggested. The blueblood composer was a workaholic who produced an important body of work, while emerging as one of the great pedagogues of his day.
ABOVE: *D'Indy photographed at his work table around 1910.*

bande à Franck: Ernest Chausson, Henri Duparc, Alexis de Castillon, Augusta Holmès, Guy Ropartz, and Guillaume Lekeu.

In *Der Ring des Niebelungen* and, even more, *Parsifal* Vincent d'Indy experienced another revelation. From Wagner he adopted such original departures as the notion of musical drama, as well as the increasingly shared belief that a work should be deeply rooted in national traditions. It followed, therefore, that the Vivarais would become the great source of inspiration for Vincent d'Indy. In 1875, during the grand fête given at Chabret in honor of his marriage to his cousin, Isabelle de Pampelonne, d'Indy took careful note of the popular air being sung by the country folk. The song would re-emerge in *Attendez-moi sous l'orme*, a little comic opera that had its premiere in 1882. A year earlier d'Indy had already composed his celebrated

The Parisian-born and -bred Vincent d'Indy did not discover the austere beauty of his family's Cévenole estate until his adolescent years. But from that moment on he made the Vivarais his favorite place in the world— and often the source of his musical inspiration.

Symphony on a French Mountain Air (Symphonie Céve-nole) to be followed in 1905 by his Third Symphony, entitled *Jour d'été à la montagne.*

In 1884 Vincent d'Indy decided to erect his own house—the Château des Faugs—several hundred meters from the old Chabret manor. With talent and infinite care, he drew up the plans himself, after which work began in 1886. The imposing edifice, built in the neo-medieval style of Viollet-le-Duc, stands on top of a steep hill, the approaches to which d'Indy had cleared to provide an unimpeded view from the heights. The raised ground floor is reached by way of broad exterior steps leading into a majestic entrance hall. This in turn opens into the living and reception rooms, all furnished in a tasteful, unostentatious manner. In addition to the inevitable piano, one of the salons contains a bookcase with wire-mesh doors and a important collection of reviews, the latter reflecting d'Indy's interest and literary participation in all the aesthetic—and political—debates of his time. The bedrooms are on the upper story, with the small one belonging to the composer located at the center of the mansion. He fitted out his office immediately above, in the mansard attic, thus assuring himself a glorious view over the valley. A veritable workaholic, d'Indy was usually at his desk well before dawn. The local newspaper reported that whenever the neighborhood children complained about getting up in the morning for school or helping with the farm work, their fathers would point to the window of *Monsieur le comte,* where the lamp had already been burning for some time.

The extremely simple furnishings of the office include a table laden with the usual objects, among them letter scales, like those owned by his contemporary Carl Nielsen, and an upright piano, an instrument for which the composer had great affection despite its mediocre quality. On the facing wall one's eye is caught by a curious arrangement of paired walking sticks horizontally aligned as if they were guns in an armory. They attest to the composer's love of taking long walks over the mountains and through the Vivarais forest. When he found a site he particularly liked d'Indy would cut a sapling, usually a pine, and make himself a cane, using the tip of his knife to carve his name and the date. Back home at Faugs, he then varnished the stick and hung it on the wall of his favorite retreat.

Vincent d'Indy never ceased talking about the rustic canes he collected during his mountain rambles. Like Vaughan Williams in England, Bartók in Hungary, Komitas in Armenia, or, in France, Canteloube in the Auvergne, Déodat de Séverac in Roussillon, and many others, d'Indy noted down ancient popular airs before they could be lost through urban emigration or the vicissitudes of history. Eventually he published several precious collections of the popular songs and peasant airs from the Vivarais.

However great his love for the land of his ancestors, Vincent d'Indy did not, by any measure, limit his oeuvre to folklore. And while *Fervaal,* his great opera, may be set in the Cévennes, it owes as much to the spirit of *Parsifal* as to peasant dances. From 1888 to 1914 d'Indy took part, as musician and lecturer, in the "Cercle des XX" in Brussels, an organization known as "Libre Esthéthique" after 1893. It was "Les XX" which,

Vincent d'Indy, who possessed a genuine talent for the plastic arts, undertook the design and decoration of his new Château des Faugs, his "dream in stone." PAGES 120–121: *The large salon* and its neo-Gothic mantelpiece. OPPOSITE: *The dining room in the Château des Faugs.*

under the direction of Antoine Maus, launched an historic series of exhibitions featuring such painters as Ensor, Rops, Seurat, Gauguin, Monet, Renoir, etc.

It may surprise some to discover d'Indy involved with these radical modernists, given his reputation as a pure, unreconstructed conservative, not only in music but also in religion and politics. His was, however, a complex and often paradoxical personality. Though a stickler capable of correcting Beethoven's faulty harmony, d'Indy also possessed a spirit large enough to embrace the music of Debussy and Ravel. This proud blueblood always refused to use his title of Count. A wealthy man, at least until the monetary erosion following World War I, he applied himself with humility and joy to all the demands of his chosen profession. At one time or another he worked as a copyist, a "piano player in various bourgeois dance halls at 25 francs a night," a drummer or horn player, parish organist (at Saint-Leu-La-Forêt), choral conductor (for Colonne and Pasdeloup), teacher (at the Conservatoire, then at the Schola Cantorum, where he became a mainstay), and musicologist (together with his friend Charles Bordes he was responsible for reviving Claudio Monteverdi and other forgotten composers in France). His pupils included Satie, Auric, Roussel, Turina, and Roland-Manuel. Vincent d'Indy sided against Captain Dreyfus; yet, he counted many Jews among his friends and edited the works of Salamone Rossi (1570– c. 1630), a Mantuan Jew known as *l'Ebreo*. Truth to tell, this affable, courteous, immensely kind man was also quite capable of making himself odious.

Isabelle d'Indy died in 1905. During the 1914– 1918 war, the composer, by then in his mid-sixties, married a young musician named Caroline Janson. Gradually he abandoned the austere Château des Faugs for L'Étrave, the villa he had built at Agay on the Mediterranean.

D'Indy also changed his musical style. In 1930 he wrote to his friend Guy Ropartz: "Now we begin our intimate period when, like Beethoven, we cannot express ourselves better than in chamber music."

Vincent d'Indy died the following year, on 2 December 1931, in his Paris apartment on the Avenue de Villars. The evening before, he had, despite his eighty-odd years, taught a regular class at the Schola Cantorum.

*A*t the Château des Faugs, Vincent d'Indy worked in a modest room at the top of the central bay overlooking the forecourt.
OPPOSITE: *The small salon with the portrait of d'Indy painted by Théo van Rysselberghe.*

TOP: *The piano in the workroom was a mediocre instrument, but greatly cherished by the composer.*
ABOVE: *A commemorative plaque presented to d'Indy by his friends in the "Cercle des XX."*

Sir Edward
Elgar

1857–1934

Edward Elgar had just turned fifty when, in 1907 and 1908, he published two orchestral suites entitled *The Wand of Youth.* The pieces were simply more developed versions of the theatre music which Elgar, as a boy of ten or twelve, had cobbled together for a little play written in collaboration with his several brothers and sisters. The sham stage sets recalled the interior of the cottage that had been the family's home at Broadheath, an isolated hamlet in the Malvern Hills above Worcester. It was here, deep in nature, that Elgar had come into the world on 2 June 1857. At the time of the playlet, the Elgars had just moved back to their former rooms over the music shop owned by the composer's father and uncle at 10 High Street in Worcester. Broadheath, however, would forever provide an essential reference point for Edward Elgar, both the man and the musician.

The work that made Elgar a household name, virtually the world over, is *Pomp and Circumstance No. 1,* a march whose noble, expansive rhythm, sonorous colors, and soaring lyricism brought glory to the coronation of King Edward VII in 1902. Legend to the contrary, however, there was nothing about this so-called "establishment" musician to place him at the center of proper Victorian or Edwardian society. Born poor and, worse, the son of a man in "trade," Elgar could never entirely escape the stigma of his lower-class origins, particularly after he married "above himself," taking as his wife Caroline Alice Roberts, who, though scarcely richer, was the daughter of a knighted army officer. Nor did Elgar belong to the musical establishment, for, amazingly enough, this composer, so sure of his means, so refined in his writing, was a pure autodidact, as he had to be, given the inability of his family to pay for the London or Leipzig education he longed for.

Elgar, furthermore, was a Roman Catholic, a condition that excluded him from the lucrative and honorific posts available in the ecclesiastical institutions of Anglican Britain. As a result, he would long earn his

way by giving violin lessons, while also playing in local orchestras and choir festivals throughout the Midlands. In 1879 he even hired himself out as a bandmaster at the Worcester county lunatic asylum, where his salary for the entire year was thirty-two pounds, plus five shillings for each polka or quadrille he composed. The struggle for survival left Elgar little time in which to develop his more important musical projects. Thus, when recognition came it was relatively late; yet, it was also sudden, triggered in 1899 by the London premiere of the *"Enigma" Variations*—fourteen subtle, poetic

*E*lgar was the principal architect of what has been called the "Renaissance" of English music that flowered during the last decade of the nineteenth century. The great composer was remarkable for his lyricism and the beauty of his sonorous colors.
OPPOSITE: *The house in Broadheath where the composer was born.*
ABOVE: *Portrait of Sir Edward Elgar by May Grafton (1909).*

portraits of familiar personalities, including Caroline Alice and the composer himself. In 1900, following two performances of *The Dream of Gerontius* in Düsseldorf, Richard Strauss hailed Elgar as the foremost English composer of the day. Two years later the freshly minted celebrity became Sir Edward Elgar, the beneficiary of a knighthood bestowed by Edward VII.

The title *Wand* refers to what the Elgar children called their parents' "imaginary despotic rule," at the same time that it also connotes the magic wand of fairies so beloved by English children and, by semantic association, a walking cane or a pilgrim's staff. For Elgar it conjured as well the cottage in Broadheath, to which he would always return throughout his life, in person or in thought. From 1912 to 1921 Elgar lived in a tall, red-brick house in Hampstead (London), the better to meet the demands of his flourishing career, but not without frequent sojourns in his native Worcestershire. And when circumstances kept him away, his imagination served to take him back. In 1917 Elgar wrote to a dear friend, Lady Alice Stuart-Wortley, daughter of the Pre-Raphaelite painter John Everett Millais: "So you have been to B[roadheath]. I fear you did not find the cottage—it is nearer the clump of Scotch firs—I

can smell them now—in the hot sun. Oh! how cruel that I was not there—there, *nothing* between that infancy & now and I want to see it. The flowers are lovely—I knew you wd. like the heath. I could have shown you such lovely lanes."

Elgar would never live in Broadheath. The cottage that is now carefully preserved, together with its mementos, would have been entirely too small to accommodate Edward, Caroline Alice, their daughter Carice, their dogs, and the whole panoply attendant upon the life of a professional and vigorously productive composer. Space was required not only for the comfortable furniture favored by the British middle classes, but also for a billiard table, a large and handsome library, and the chemistry laboratory in which the composer, like his contemporary Sherlock Holmes, engaged in

"*S*o you have been to B[roadheath]. I fear you did not find the cottage—it is nearer the clump of Scotch firs—I can smell them now—in the hot sun. . . . The flowers are lovely— I knew you wd. like the heath."

OPPOSITE: *Elgar's violin and the score of* Salut d'Amour, *one of his first successes.*
ABOVE: *The Elgar children's playhouse at Broadheath.*

often malodorous experiments—i.e., explosives. Another proud possession was the big gramophone, a modern invention that Elgar loved from the start; indeed, by the end of his life he could hear recordings of almost everything he had ever written.

If one stuck a pin into a map at every one of the numerous sites where Elgar chose to reside, the pins would form a sort of magic circle around Broadheath. From 1891 to 1899 there was "Forli," a house at Malvern Link, where Elgar composed his Serenade in E minor, *Scenes from the Bavarian Highlands, The Light of Life (Lux Christi)* oratorio, and the *"Enigma" Variations.* In 1899 the Elgars moved again, this time to Malvern itself, where they occupied a beautiful house that Edward, who adored riddles, called "Craeg Lea," an anagram of his own surname. As a substitute for Broadheath, the

In reality, Elgar left Broadheath at a very early age. The furniture and other objects now there came from other Elgar residences.

Still, the composer never wandered far or long from this tiny hamlet in the Malvern Hills, for him the center of the universe.

composer also rented "Birchwood," a house situated well off the beaten path in the Malvern Hills. From this period date *Pomp and Circumstance;* the *Sea Pictures* song cycle; *The Dream of Gerontius* oratorio, based upon the eponymous poem by Cardinal Newman; and *Caractacus,* a cantata celebrating the British chieftain whose brave defense of his land against the Romans prompted Emperor Claudius to spare his life in C. AD 50.

In 1904, however, the Elgars abandoned Craeg Lea, after a construction project threatened to deprive them of their view of the Severn Valley. Now they landed near Hereford at "Plâs Gwyn," a far more luxurious dwelling that reflected the improved circumstances the family would henceforth enjoy. Indeed, one biographer has characterized Plâs Gwyn as "a little Potsdam." Here the composer wrote three of his most important masterpieces—the two symphonies and the violin concerto. Elgar was also invited to become Mayor of Hereford, an honor he refused, which may seem ironic given the sometime view of him as an "official" musician.

After his London period—sadly darkened by the 1914–1918 war, the collapse of the old order (a pathetic echo of which can be heard in the Cello Concerto), and the death of Lady Elgar in 1920—the aging composer returned to Worcestershire. Even then, he went on regularly changing his address, always in the enchanted circle around Broadheath: "Napleton Grange" along the Severn (1923–1927), "Battenham Manor" near Worcester (1927–1928), then a house in Tiddington near Stratford-on-Avon (1928–1929), and, finally, "Marl Bank" on a hilltop in Worcester.

After his wife died, Elgar produced relatively little original work, but the *Severn Suite* of 1930 and the *Nursery Suite* of 1931 are nonetheless memorable creations. To the end of his days the composer would be haunted by the world in which he grew up. He died at "Marl Bank" on 23 February 1934. Shortly thereafter, Carice Elgar sketched a word portrait of her father, declaring that no one had ever been more imbued with the spirit and essence of his native countryside. For him Worcestershire was everything, its cottages, gardens, fields, and orchards like none other in the world.

Sir Edward Elgar rests in the little Catholic cemetery at the Church of St. Wulstan near Little Malvern.

From his grave visitors can see a good part of the magic circle. In 1931, when King George V made him a peer of the realm, with the title of Baronet, Sir Edward, without a moment's hesitation, chose to be styled the first Lord Broadheath, Bt.

"*T*his is the best of me; for the rest, I ate, and drank, and slept, loved and hated, like another; my life was as the vappur and is not; but this I saw and knew; this, if anything of mine, is worth your memory." *John Ruskin, quoted by Elgar at the end of* The Dream of Gerontius.

Giacomo
Puccini

1858–1924

Pilgrims to sites where Giacomo Puccini lived and labored do not have to venture very far from Lucca, the city of his birth, at 30 Via di Poggio, on 2 December 1858. Yet, Puccini was a frequent long-distance traveler who visited every part of Europe, as well as North and South America, even Egypt, for reasons of both pleasure and profession. Absence, however, simply made him grow fonder of his native ground, situated in the extreme northwest corner of Tuscany, between the Mediterranean and the Alps. "Yes," he wrote, "in the wild, green, rustic expanse of the splendid Maremme—hospitable soil for decent people—I spend, I do believe, the most beautiful days of my life. Following a success, how could I do better than go hunting in nature when the game is good."

The Puccini family originated in Celle, a hamlet in the beautiful Serchio Valley near Pescaglia in the Tuscan Apennines. For the Puccinis, as for the Bach, Scarlatti, and Couperin dynasties, music constituted a natural birthright. From the early eighteenth century, four generations of Puccinis had succeeded one another as music directors at San Martino Cathedral in Lucca: Jacopo (1712–1781), Antonio-Benedetto Maria (1747–1832), Domenico (1771–1815), and Michele (1812–1864), the father of Giacomo.

Giacomo Puccini appears therefore to have been preordained for a career in music. Beginning as a choirboy at the age of ten, he advanced to organist at fourteen, before launching into organ composition at sixteen. This was, however, the century of Italian opera, which made it all but inevitable that Giacomo would be more drawn to the theatre than to the Church. In 1876, after attending a performance of *Aïda* in Pisa—where, for the want of money, he had walked the thirty-two kilometers from Lucca—young Puccini decided to break with family tradition. The process began with courses at the Pacini Institute in Lucca, followed by further study at the Milan Conservatory, Italy's most prestigious music school. In 1883 Puccini

entered *Le Villi*, his one-act opera/ballet, in a competition staged by Edoardo Sonzogno to help young composers display their talents. Puccini failed to win the prize, his manuscript being almost eligible, but *Le Villi* caught the attention of Arrigo Boito. As a result, it was produced in the following year at Milan's Teatro dal Verme, with stunning success.

Edgar (1889), Puccini's second opera, was a flop, but, starting with *Manon Lescaut* in 1892, the composer would score one resounding hit after another, at least in public opinion, even if the critics disgraced themselves by failing to appreciate the new genius. *La Bohème* (1896), *Tosca* (1900), *Madama Butterfly* (1904), *Il Trittico* (1918), and *Turandot* (1926, premiered posthumously) mark the highlights in a career so brilliant as to compare with that of Giuseppe Verdi.

"I am a man of the theatre, I make theatre, and I am a visual person. I see the characters, the colors, and the action. If, while shut away at home, I cannot visualize the scene, there in front of me, I cannot compose, I cannot write a note."
OPPOSITE: *Puccini's "studio" at Torre del Lago.*
ABOVE: *Photographic portrait of Giacomo Puccini by Piccagliani.*

In 1884 Puccini discovered Torre del Lago, a tiny village on Lake Massaciuccoli, about twenty-five kilometers west of Lucca. With "its 120 souls and dozen houses," Torre del Lago would have held little appeal but for a magnificent view over both the lake and the mountains. Puccini, who despised cities and the worldly life, fell in love with Torre del Lago at first sight. Writing from Paris in 1898, he exclaimed: "I loathe sidewalks! I loathe buildings! I loathe the great capitals! I loathe columns!" Torre del Lago was host to nothing more than a small colony of artists, mostly rowdies and bohemians like Puccini. There, by contrast to his life in Lucca, he could live without re-

"On Lake Massaciuccoli there are ruins of baths from the time of Nero in the second century and a Roman villa. From there one can go to Torre del Lago, not for the artistic delights of the place, since it is a small modern town, but rather to visit the house of Giacomo Puccini. . . ."
Romy Grieco, Lucca città d'arte.

proach for cohabiting "in sin" with Elvira Gemigniani, the wife of a former classmate. Best of all, perhaps, Lake Massaciuccoli fairly burgeoned with ducks, waterfowl, and other feathered aquatics, all beckoning Puccini to indulge his passion for hunting, which the great composer ranked second only to music.

Puccini settled at Torre del Lago in 1891. At first he merely rented, but once the *Bohème* royalties began rolling in, he built a sober, traditional, but comfortable house. At the bottom of the garden planted with clumps of trees and palms was a gate just outside which lay the waters of the lake. It therefore took only a few steps for Puccini, guns in hand, to step into a dinghy and paddle off to his hunting cabin.

Puccini's reception/workroom takes up most of the ground floor. Like the other rooms, it is furnished in a comfortable, if somewhat "cathedral," though not charmless, manner typical of the late nineteenth

century. Inevitably, the eye is drawn to the composer's upright Förster, an instrument equipped with a special mute. Puccini always composed on the piano, with hat on head and preferably from ten at night to four in the morning. On the left of the piano, facing the window, is a small table where Puccini wrote—or, more accurately, scribbled—his scores. The second essential room is a veritable armory, now almost museum of guns and hunting boots.

At Torre del Lago Puccini often mixed with a rather wild bunch of young men, made up primarily of daubers like Francesco Pagni and Nino Marotti. Others, such as Angiolino Tommasi and Plinio Nomellini,

The large number of paintings and drawings in the villa's "gallery" remind us that most of Puccini's friends around Torre del Lago were painters, drawn there by the poetic, shifting light along the lake shore.

would actually earn a modicum of national recognition. These roistering characters, all with big appetites for both food and drink, hung out in a sort of inn maintained by the local cobbler. Named the *Capanna di Giovanni delle Bande Nere* ("Giovanni of the Black Stripes"), it would soon be redubbed the "Club La Bohème." The rules said much about its prevailing spirit: "Poker faces, pedants, weak stomachs, blockheads, puritans, and similar blackguards need not apply and will be driven away without mercy." As for Articles 6, 7, and 8, they decreed: "All games permitted by law are prohibited. Remaining quiet is prohibited. Moderation is prohibited, except in special cases."

From his outpost at Torre del Lago, Giacomo Puccini, who adored speed, pursued several of his favorite sports: bicycle riding, racing on the lake in *Ricochet*, his motorboat, and touring about in a "sidecar" or an automobile. An early fan of the motorcar, he

would own several, one of which almost cost him his life when it crashed in 1903.

Despite these distractions, it was along the shore of Lake Massaciuccoli that Puccini composed most of his masterpieces. Their limited number, at least in relation to the prodigious output of a Donizetti or a Verdi, was not for the lack of enterprise on the part of the author. Puccini simply worked very slowly; moreover, he often began projects only to drop them soon thereafter.

In 1898 Puccini had a house erected in the Monsagrati Hills near Chiatri, but Elvira detested the place, and the couple spent little time there. Later, the composer bought another villa, at Boscolungo in the Tuscan Apennines above Pistoia, where he wrote part of *Madama Butterfly*. For the quietude he needed in order to complete this opera, Puccini even retired temporarily to the old family home in Celle. All the while, however, it was Torre del Lago that claimed the heart of a man who, in conjugal matters, never regarded fidelity as a major virtue. "Torre del Lago," he wrote, "supreme joy, paradise, Eden, the Empyrean, *turris eburnea, vas spiritualis,* my kingdom. . . ." Furthermore, the powerful automobiles favored by the maestro made child's play of the short distances between Monsagrati, Boscolungo, Celle, Lucca (where part of the Puccini family still lived), and the favorite hideout: Torre del Lago.

By the end of 1921, however, Puccini felt compelled to abandon Torre del Lago. Industrial "civilization" had finally caught up with the village, fouled by a noisy peat factory. For several years Puccini had owned land in the great pine forest of Viareggio, then a small fishing port well off the tourist route and known to the world only as the place where the English poet Shelley had drowned. It was here that the composer decided to build his new house. Less than eight kilometers from Torre del Lago, Viareggio made it possible for Puccini to enjoy his "paradise" without suffering any of the recent problems. The new villa, which would be pillaged during World War II, was considerably more sumptuous than its predecessor, and Puccini became quite attached to it. The proximity of the sea even prompted him to acquire a yacht, christened the *Cio-Cio-San* in honor of *Madama Butter-*

fly, but he soon had to give it up because of the "barrels and barrels" of fuel consumed by the vessel even for the briefest voyage.

It was at Viareggio—as well as in a hunting lodge deep in the Tuscan Maremme—that Puccini undertook his last masterpiece, *Turandot.* The final two scenes were merely sketched in when the throat cancer afflicting the composer took a sudden turn for the worse. In search of treatment, he traveled to Brussels, where he died on 29 September 1924.

Puccini is buried in the Torre del Lago villa, in a tomb within the thickness of the wall dividing the workroom from the armory, between his piano and his guns.

"*F*ollowing a success, how could I do better than go hunting in nature when the game is good," asked Puccini, who did just that on every possible occasion, even after a failure.
ABOVE: *The armory at Torre del Lago.*

Carl
Nielsen
1865–1931

Nestled between the Jutland peninsula and great Zealand, Fyn is the second largest island in Denmark, and it may be the Viking nation's most characteristic province. Here, for instance, were born both Hans Christian Andersen (1805–1875) and Carl Nielsen, two luminaries who, for the world at large, symbolize Danish civilization at its best. Andersen came into the world at Odense, Fyn's principal city, and Nielsen a dozen kilometers farther south, near the hamlet of Sortelung in the parish district of Nørre-Lyndelse on 9 June 1865. The storyteller and the composer alike sprang from very modest families. Carl Nielsen's father, a smalltime house painter as well as the village musician, regularly played trumpet and violin at weddings, baptisms, and other peasant celebrations. According to Carl, the man known as "Niels the painter" possessed "a rare sense of rhythm and played with such a steady beat that it could have been the pistons of a steam-driven motor. This is what made him the best dance fiddler in the whole of central Fyn."

Like Hans Christian Andersen in *My Rural Childhood,* Carl Nielsen wrote a book of memoirs describing his youth: "At the age of eight or nine, I studied the violin with my father and with Professor [Emil] Petersen [the local schoolmaster], and I composed my first songs." Before long he would be tending livestock in the afternoon and accompanying or substituting for his father at evening festivities in the village.

After a brief stint as a grocery salesman, young Nielsen, having just turned fourteen, competed for and easily won a job as army musician. "I quickly became one of the best buglers in the regiment," he wrote. "I had the lips, firm and not too thick, my teeth were perfectly aligned to fit the bugle's mouthpiece, and I could hold the high notes for almost a minute. All this, of course, had nothing to do with music, but rather with a sport useful to a young man eager to prove himself, and at the time it afforded me the self-

confidence I very much needed given that I did not shine in anything else."

Here Carl Nielsen protests rather too much, for, in fact, the people of Odense recognized his musical gifts almost immediately. In May 1883, a group of local music lovers, encouraged by the Nielson family, pledged the money making it possible for Carl to attend the Conservatory in Copenhagen, where he studied with Niels Gade (1817–1890), the most famous Danish composer of the period. In 1888, following graduation, young Nielsen introduced, in the concert hall at the famous Tivoli Gardens, his Opus 1, the *Little Suite* for strings. The popularity of this work has not diminished

"*C*arl Nielsen was a born symphonist—even though his production extended to all musical styles. One often speaks of the head and the heart— Carl Nielsen possessed both, in the highest degree."
—Jean Sibelius.
OPPOSITE: *The house in which Carl Nielsen grew up.*
ABOVE: *Photographic portrait of Carl Nielsen (1920s).*

"*I spent the last two weeks of December at the house, with my parents and some of my brothers and sisters. The pig had been slaughtered, and Papa had only chickens left.*

The two pear trees in the garden were stiff with frost and refused to admit that once upon a time Albert and I had shaken the ripe fruit from their branches."

even today. In the same year Nielsen joined the violin section of the Royal Orchestra, and in 1905 he assumed the post of conductor. Meanwhile, a travel grant allowed him to make a grand tour of Europe. While in Paris, Nielsen met a young sculptress, Anne Marie Brodersen, whom he married in Florence in May 1891. The union, which joined two artists with strong personalities, would have to weather a number of domestic storms, but it never foundered.

In his heart, and perhaps even more in his ear, Carl Nielsen always remained deeply rooted in his native soil: "On Fyn nothing is as elsewhere, and anyone who takes the trouble to listen will realize it. Even the bees buzz in a special way, with a particular Fynian accent; the horses whinny and the russet cows moo differently than elsewhere in the country. The thrush sings a Fynian melody, and the laughter of the blackbird, when darting in and out of the lilac groves, sounds like the song of the starling, which in turn imitates the ravishing babble of young florentines playing and giggling behind the trimmed garden hedges. The bells ring and the cocks crow in Fynian, and from the birds' nests bursts an almost symphonic joy every time the mother returns to feed her young. Everything sings in the same key, and even the trees dream and speak in their dreams in the Fynian language."

It should not be assumed, however, that Nielsen was a folklorist or even a composer of "program" music. Although his numerous Danish songs remain true models of the genre, his other masterpieces, notably the six symphonies, the three concertos (for violin, for flute, and for clarinet), and the two operas, *Saul og David* (1898–1901) and *Maskarade* (1904–1906), reveal a distinctly personal quality, transcending labels but often fusing the most diverse kinds of musical language. The Fifth Symphony, for example, contains an early touch of the aleatory, requiring a drummer to improvise so as to drown the rest of the orchestra. For Nielsen, therefore, Fyn is primarily a spiritual domain. And this remains true despite the debt his rhythmic genius owed to Fynian dances, or his taste for a kind of modal writing common to many composers enthralled by nature.

At the end of a life devoid of history outside music, Carl Nielsen died on 3 October 1931 in Copenhagen, where he had never ceased to reside. Today,

Born into a modest family, then quickly acclaimed, Nielsen never let celebrity go to his head. This can be seen in the comfortable but unpretentious setting in which he chose to live.

however, it is Odense which offers a twofold reward for those interested in the composer.

First, there is the house in which the Nielsens lived until 1891, and now carefully preserved as the place the young musician left when he departed for the Danish capital. The white-painted brick cottage, with its steep, heavily thatched roof, sits just off the road from Ostense to Fåborg, free of the half-timbering characteristic of many Fynian dwellings. The relative vastness reflects the size of the Nielsen brood, which, in Carl's generation, included a total of twelve children. The large, substantial house also bears witness to a certain improvement in the financial state of "Niels the painter" during the 1870s. Several years earlier, about the time Carl was born, the Nielsens had shared with another family "a small peasant cottage in the middle of a field." Among the memorabilia displayed at Nørre-Lyndelse is an especially touching photograph; it portrays a young regimental musician clad in a flat cap and a uniform too large for his slender frame, a bugle in one hand and in the other a

trombone, the latter waist high even though set on the ground.

Second, there are two rooms—the studio and the main parlor—from the Copenhagen apartment in which Nielsen lived until 1915, both reconstituted by the citizens of Odense in the outbuildings of the town's beautiful concert hall. Anne Marie Nielsen kept a separate atelier at a different location. The parlor lacks nothing, yet nothing is superfluous. The rigor of the polished, straight-legged furniture is relieved only by the variety of the paintings and sculptures, among which figures a large bronze dog by Anne Marie Nielsen. The music room offers greater warmth and welcome. Like the parlor, it abounds in pictures and objets d'art from every period. A large Baroque-style tapestry hangs above the bed where the composer slept during his long nights of work. Behind the Hornung and Møller grand piano, with its two square benches, rests a double music stand, reminding us that Nielsen's instrument was, above all, the violin— the bugle and trombone notwithstanding. No useless bibelot here either, nothing in excess, not even the few implements casually spread across the desk, along with random piles of well-thumbed scores. One device —the postal scale—is a relic of a well-documented passion for writing letters. The musician's youngest daughter, Anne Marie Telmànyi, who, in a painting of the Copenhagen apartment, portrayed her father writing or composing at this desk, his back straight, even a bit stiff as in most photographs of him. Nielsen was a simple, shy man, and if one may judge by a present he received in 1925 on his sixtieth birthday—a superb silk dressing gown!—he was also as much a homebody as his music was bold, evolved, and expansive.

Carl Nielsen seldom had the time to visit his native Fyn. He made a pilgrimage there in 1925, with his brother Albert, a photographer established in Chicago. Still, he never stopped thinking about the island. In 1921 he dedicated *Fynsk foraar (Springtime on Fyn)*, one of his most beautiful a capella choruses, to Fyn, and in a 1927 issue of *Musique vivante* he confessed that "the Fynian country does not change; it remains firmly and securely where, after sweet and serious reflection, it decided to drop anchor. How calmly and gracefully it slipped in between Jutland and Zealand. . . . Who

could resist its magic, in which all is complete harmony and everlasting? Is it true, as we are told, that love is blind? In any event, I have never heard that it is deaf. . . ."

*T*he capstone of the Nielsen oeuvre unquestionably consists of the six symphonies, several of them with signifying titles: The Four Temperaments (No. 2), Sinfonia espansiva (No. 3), The Inextinguishable (No. 4), and Sinfonia semplice (No. 6). ABOVE: *A Pièta by Anne Marie Nielsen.*

Jean
Sibelius
1865–1957

But for Jean Sibelius, the village of Järvenpää, some forty kilometers north of Helsinki, would very likely never have emerged from obscurity. It was here, on a wooded hill near the center of Finland, that the great composer chose to build the house he would live in for almost half a century. The sheer beauty of the site had prompted the painter Eero Järnefelt to bring Sibelius, his brother-in-law, for an outing on skis. Immediately delighted with what he saw, the musician ordered construction begun in the spring of 1904, and by the following September he and his family had already moved in.

Jean Sibelius—his first name taken from a French uncle—was born on 8 December 1865 in Hämeenlinna, a small garrison town where his father served as the military physician. Finland, with all its racial, linguistic, and cultural peculiarities, had for centuries been fought over by Sweden and Russia. For the moment it was under tsarist domination. Jean began studying the violin with the director of the military band in Hämeenlinna, and it did not take long for his remarkable gifts to emerge, making him appear destined for a career as a soloist or a composer. In 1885, when his secondary studies had been completed, the Sibelius

family insisted that their son study law. A year later, however, Jean abandoned the idea of becoming a lawyer and enrolled at the Helsinki Conservatory, studying composition under the great Finnish teacher Martin Wegelius (1846–1906). During his four years at the Conservatory, Sibelius had the opportunity to make friends with Ferruccio Busoni, a few months younger but already famous for his pianistic virtuosity and bold transcriptions.

After two years of polishing his talents in Berlin, Sibelius returned to Finland in 1891. He now commenced a series of works based upon the poems of the *Kalevala*, Finland's great national epic. Beginning with the oratorio *Kullervo* and the symphonic poem *En Saga* (1892), the *Kalevala* scores placed Sibelius in the front rank of Finish composers. The first of his symphonies had its premiere in April 1899, the success of which

The popular Valse Triste— *actually an excerpt from a score for theatre music—represents no more than a tiny branch in Jean Sibelius's magnificent forest of works, one of the most important* *bodies of music created around the turn of the century.* ABOVE: *Portrait of Jean Sibelius sketched by Albert Edelpelt during the same year the composer moved to Järvenpää.*

The Silence of Järvenpää

would be surpassed, in November of the same year, by the *Scènes historiques*. The stunning triumph of this work was both musical and political. It arrived in the wake of Tsar Nicholas II's "February Manifesto," which abolished the relative autonomy the Grand Duchy of Finland had enjoyed within the Russian Empire. The Manifesto also severely limited the fundamental liberties long claimed by the people of Finland. In this oppressive climate the *Scènes historiques*—particularly the sixth tableau, today famous as *Finlandia*—was certain to enflame passions and transform the composer into a national hero.

Before long Sibelius had become famous all over Europe, where he began making tours. In this period he also composed the celebrated *Valse triste* (sold to the publisher Breitkopf & Härtel for the ridiculous

Jean Sibelius once dreamt of a career as a virtuoso violinist, and his concerto for that instrument is a great classic of the genre.

For the piano, however, he composed some thirty volumes of pieces.

sum of 300 marks), the less well-known Violin Concerto (1903), and the Second Symphony (1902).

In 1892 Sibelius had married Aino, the daughter of General Alexander Järnefelt, then well known for his nationalist convictions. By 1904 the couple had already produced three children, and the composer was going through a troubled period. Despite his successes, Sibelius was in serious financial trouble, brought on by lavish spending and over-indulgence in alcohol and tobacco. Finding it impossible to work in Helsinki, he decided to settle in Järvenpää, on the property he called "Ainola" in honor of both his wife and the legendary heroine of the *Kalevala*.

During his numerous tours, Jean Sibelius loved to live in grand style. Back at Ainola, however, he preferred Finnish simplicity. The parlor was rarely used except when visitors called.

The house was built by Sibelius's friend Lars Sonk, a renowned architect who would also design the summer residence of republican Finland's President and several of the nation's religious structures. Ainola is a typical all-wood Finnish cottage, in which beams and lathwork are generally left exposed. Most of the furniture—sober and extremely comfortable—reflects the taste of middle-class Finnish families at the turn of the century. The radio, of which Sibelius was a passionate consumer, figured large in this ensemble. On the ground floor a huge bay window admits a flood of light into the dining room, its space further warmed by a superb fireplace clad in green tiles. On this level too is the parlor, long used merely as an office, where Sibelius composed his Third Symphony (1906), among other works. It was here that the great man received his guests, and placed the beautiful Steinway given

him on the occasion of his fiftieth birthday in 1915, just as he was completing the first version of his Fifth Symphony. The family generally gathered in the adjacent library, especially for the daily ritual of going through the mail. Sibelius, a man very open to the world and a dedicated user of both telephone and telegraph, received a massive amount of post, which often included boxes of cigars sent by admirers aware of his appetites. During World War II Prime Minister Churchill himself arranged for the composer to be supplied with his favorite tobacco. Also worth noting on the ground floor is the vast kitchen, a witness to the fact that Sibelius was a practiced gourmand, who loved food in general but oysters and wild duck in particular.

A wooden stairway leads to the upper storey added by Sibelius in 1911. Here he fitted out his bedroom and the studio in which he created many of his works. The atelier offers a view over the forests of birch and pine all the way to Lake Tuusula. At the foot of the house Aino Sibelius, an enthusiastic horticulturist, laid out a magnificent garden, complete with a hothouse in which tomatoes could ripen, at a mere five degrees off the Arctic Circle. At Järvenpää nature, which Sibelius adored, reigned supreme.

Until 1914 Sibelius traveled a very great deal, in the course of which he received many honors, from France, Britain, Austria/Hungary, and the United States. The Great War, however, fell heavily on Järvenpää, where Sibelius could no longer receive royalties from his German publishers, Breitkopf & Härtel. After the Russian Revolution, Communists attempted to seize power in Finland, and during the civil war that followed, Sibelius had to flee Ainola and seek refuge in the hospital where his brother was head physician.

Finally, on 17 July 1919, the Republic of Finland was proclaimed. With this Sibelius became, in the eyes of the world, the foremost symbol of Finish national genius.

Sibelius now resumed his wandering life as a celebrated composer and conductor. The Sixth and Seventh Symphonies (1924, 1926) and the beautiful symphonic poem *Tapiola* are the crowning works of the period. After *Tapiola*, however, Sibelius almost stopped composing. He even destroyed his Eighth Symphony, a work actually finished in 1929.

Sibelius still had left to him many long years of life, which he spent peacefully at Ainola in the company of his wife, five daughters, grandchildren, friends, and countless vistors, the famous and the anonymous all greeted with kindness and modesty. For his ninetieth

*F*innish art is everywhere evident at Ainola. In music, however, Sibelius "did not imitate, adapt, or utilize folklore. He created a personal style, which allied the modality of folklore with the tonality of learned music." Erkki Salmenhaara.

birthday, the composer received more than 1,200 telegrams. Sibelius died on 20 September 1957 in his house, three months before his ninety-second birthday. He is buried in the park at Ainola, under a simple stone surrounded by the trees he loved so much.

His death brought an end to thirty years lived without fanfare but with much happiness in "the silence of Järvenpää."

The substantial kitchen reflects the composer's epicurean temperament, as well as the number of people—large family, loyal friends, frequent guests—who broke bread at Ainola.
LEFT: *The villa's porch.*

Franz
Lehár
1870–1948

Ischl may date back to ancient times, as a Roman in-
scription attests, but the little town in Austria's Salzkammergut remained virtually unknown to the world
at large until the early decades of the nineteenth
century. This was the so-called "Biedermeier" period,
during which Archduke Franz Karl and Archduchess
Sophie discovered Ischl and its charms: the peaceful
ensemble of lakes, mountains, and forests, the shim-
mering course of the River Traun, and, most of all, the
mineral springs. The presumed therapeutic benefits of
consuming or bathing in these warm waters transformed Ischl into a spa, known ever since as Bad Ischl.

   For the archducal couple's son, Emperor Franz
Joseph, Bad Ischl became a place of enchantment.
Born in 1830, Franz Joseph would reign for almost
three-quarters of a century, from 1848 until his death
in 1916. Throughout this time he never ceased to frequent Bad Ischl, primarily for the game-rich forests in
which he could indulge his passion for the sport of
kings. During the high season—that is, summer—Bad

Ischl served as the de facto capital of Austria, a magnet
for everyone who counted in the Austro/Hungarian
Empire—ministers, courtesans, artists. The resort also
attracted Sissi von Wittelsbach, the ravishing, dark-
haired Bavarian Princess with whom Franz Joseph fell
madly in love. The Café Zauner—epicenter of fashionable life—teemed with writers like Grillparzer and
Wedekind, the favorite painters of the day, the beautiful dancer Fanny Eissler, and, of course, the reigning
stars of the musical scene: Meyerbeer, Brahms, Bruck-
ner, Hugo Wolf, Johann II and Oscar Strauss, Nicolaï
(who wrote *The Merry Wives of Windsor* at Bad Ischl),
and Suppé, among others.

*Lehár, along with Johann
Strauss II and Jules Offenbach,
raised operetta to the level of a
proper musical genre. His last
operetta, Giuditta (1934), was
in fact written for the prestigious
Vienna State Opera.*

   *It may surprise some to learn
that Lehár was approached to*

*complete Turandot, the grand
opera Puccini left unfinished
at his death?*
ABOVE: *Franz Lehár in 1894,
uniformed for his role as
conductor of the Imperial Naval
Band stationed at Pula on
Croatia's Adriatic coast.*

Traunquai 8, Bad Ischl

Meanwhile, another, humbler musician was struggling to capture his moment of glory. Franz Lehár was born in Komáron, Hungary, on 30 April 1870. The son of a military bandmaster, he spent his childhood being dragged from garrison to garrison. Having become an excellent violinist by the age of twelve, Franz was sent for further training at the Prague Conservatory. There he studied composition with Fibich and received advice from Dvorák, while also mastering the usual curriculum. At eighteen, he did his military service in music with the Fiftieth Infantry, and then followed the paternal example by remaining in the army, as a conductor of regimental music in a variety of places. In 1896 Lehár resigned from the military with the idea of making his reputation in opera. When this failed, he immediately went back into uniform. Only in 1902 did

The entrance hall at Villa-Lehár opens on to the narrow, tree-lined quay along the rapid waters of the River Traun. Here furniture, objets d'art, and trophies of various styles and origins have been combined, often with wry wit.

the Viennese success of his marches and waltzes—particularly *Gold and Silver*—allow the Hungarian musician to achieve an independent career.

Lehár's first operettas garnered mixed reviews, but then came *Die lustige Witwe*, which opened on 30 December 1905 at the Theater an der Wien. *The Merry Widow*, as English-speakers know the work, survived to become the most successful operetta of all time. With *The Count of Luxembourg* (1909) and *Gypsy Love* (1910), which followed soon thereafter, the one-time army bandmaster found himself revelling in universal glory. Now Lehár could afford to purchase the Bad Ischl villa of Princess von Sabran at Traunquai 8, today renamed Franz-Lehár-quai. There he spent long months every year until his death on 24 October 1948.

The "Villa-Lehár," with its Classical forms, elegant proportions, and spacious but human scale, is beautifully situated. The Hotel Elizabeth, then the most exclusive hostelry in Bad Ischl, faced the Lehár dwelling on the opposite side of the river. It could be reached by way of a bridge over the Traun, which was close enough for convenience and yet sufficiently distant for the noise of its traffic to be muted. From the Elizabeth it took only a few minutes to reach the Café

Zauner, where, if a period photograph is to be believed, "the ladies, the ladies, the ladies" serenaded in *The Merry Widow* were undoubtedly eager to sit at the composer's feet.

Entrance to the Villa-Lehár is through a large door opening on to the tree-lined quay or, more

The opulence of the parlor floor says much about the success of The Merry Widow. *In 1935 Franz Lehár became the publisher of what was almost a complete edition of his works.*
ABOVE: *Behind the Steinway*

grand piano, which serves as a pedestal for a Gallé vase, Lehár hung the portrait of Hélène Odilon surrounded by the bronze-dipped laurel crowns collected in the course of his long career.

intimately, through the cool garden laid out alongside the house. On the interior one is instantly struck by the personal quality of the décor. The rooms, despite their opulence, are neither pompous nor pretentious, thanks to the freshness of the wall materials and the clarity of the overall arrangement. As a theatre man sophisticated in the art of performance, Lehár knew how to re-create at home the light-hearted spirit of his operettas, which were at antipodal remove from the "bear-skin" heaviness of German grand opera. The same effect arises from the quite particular way in which the composer organized his vast collection of furniture, paintings, sculptures, and bibelots from every period and provenance. Instead of classifying items by era or genre, as in a museum, Lehár presented them according to his own fancy, in combinations designed for maximum visual appeal.

Wherever the eye turns it may discover, all mixed together as in the large hall, an armoir from a Tyrolean sacristy, silk tapestries from the Orient, and hunting trophies too beautiful to be real. In the dining room decorated with vividly colored Meissen plates, one can almost smell the subtle aroma of gourmand cuisine. The huge studio is on the upper storey, where Lehár composed many of his works, inspired, as he said, by the air of Bad Ischl. On the wall, not far from the Steinway grand embellished with a superb Gallé vase, Lehár hung, somewhat asymmetrically, a dozen bronze-dipped laurel wreaths collected in the course of his career. With wit and modesty, he grouped them around not a portrait of himself but rather that of Hélène Odilon, wife of the famous operetta singer Alexander Girardi.

Also found on this level is the reception room, pleasantly extended by a veranda overlooking the river. Here, too, disparate styles and genres flirt with one another, in a gamut running from kitsch tables laden with medallions to a *Drunken Silenus* attributed to Van Dyck. As elsewhere in the villa, the room benefits from the merry presence of a tall stove made of glistening white ceramic, a feature typical of Central Europe. This refined though unfussy ambiance continues on the floor above, where the composer fitted out his smoking room, a small, intimate parlor, and another studio or workroom reserved for correspondence.

For four decades Lehár delivered an almost un-

broken string of hits, the most sparkling of which were *Paganini* (1925), *Gigolette* (1926), *Tsarevitch* (1927), and, especially, *The Land of Smiles* (1929). When moving pictures arrived, he immediately got involved with the medium, for which he not only adapted some of his stage works but also composed several original scores. At Bad Ischl, meanwhile, Lehár lived through the turbulent drama of Austria/Hungary, the carefree decadence of the Empire, and the terrible 1914–1918 war. In 1918 came the dismemberment of the Habsburg empire and in 1936 the *Anschluss*. By a stroke of bad luck, *The Merry Widow* happened to be a great favorite of Adolf Hitler, whose reverence for Wagner, by contrast, was merely a pose for political effect. Lehár, despite his wife's being Jewish, never had the courage to emigrate. After the collapse of the Third Reich, he was accused of having remained passive in the face of evil, but the ostracism did not last long, given that he had never been involved in politics.

Lehár left his house to Bad Ischl, on condition that the city maintain the villa just as it was during his lifetime.

*T*he topmost storey in Villa-Lehár was fitted out for private life—card games, cigars among friends, correspondence, and sleep.

PAGES 164–165: *The small parlor upstairs.*
ABOVE: *The composer's bedroom.*

Maurice Ravel

1875–1937

Visitors to Maurice Ravel's house atop Montfort-l'Amaury are in for a surprise, once they have climbed the hill leading up from the Place de l'Église and glimpsed the so-called "Belvédère." They may already know that royalties from *Boléro* have beaten every record for almost three-quarters of a century, or that this small town—onetime citadel of Simon de Montfort on the edge of the Rambouillet Forest—abounds in sumptuous residences. They may also recall photographs of Ravel, always an elegant man who, in his youth, was even considered a dandy. Very likely their heads resonate with the composer's music—*Gaspard de la nuit*, *Daphnis et Chloé*, the String Quartet in F. Then suddenly, on their left, they discover what Manuel Rosenthal, Ravel's pupil and friend, described as "a sort of little pavilion, not even a villa, a bit like a badly cut slice of Camembert—built of very poor materials."

In April 1921, when he acquired the Belvédère, at 5 Avenue Saint-Laurent (today Rue Maurice Ravel), the composer was preparing to settle in one place for the first, and last, time in his life. During his forty-two years, he had lived with his parents, moved with them on eight different occasions, traveled extensively, made frequent stays at Saint-Jean-de-Luz, and served during the 1914–1918 war as a stretcher-bearer at Verdun. After the death of his mother in 1917, Ravel had moved in with friends. Finally, a modest inheritance, rather than royalties, allowed him "to inquire about a little shack some thirty kilometers, at least, from Paris." *Faute de mieux* because, as he also wrote to Georgette Marnold in March 1920, "I sometimes dream of a wonderful convent in Spain, but, without faith, it would be completely idiotic."

Actually, Ravel paid relatively little for the "little shack": 20,000 old francs, that is, about 833 dollars or 520 pounds sterling in today's money. Other reasons for his choice were the two gardens (a pleasure garden and two parcels offering a kitchen garden and an

orchard), the possibility of walks in the Rambouillet Forest, and, perhaps most of all, a magnificent view—the "Belvédère"—over Montfort-l'Amaury and the valley below.

From 1921 to 1927 Ravel worked endlessly to transform the house. He added two wings, increased the number of rooms from four to eight, and built a small interior stairway from the living rooms to the bedroom and bath located at the garden level above. Until 1924 there had been no direct communication between the lower rooms and the rest of the house, which meant that Ravel had to brave the elements both in the morning and at bedtime. "I leave you," he wrote at the end of a letter to Roland-Manuel. "With my storm lamp in hand, I retire to my bedroom swimming through a downpour." He also had electricity

"Ravel dreams of perfection, and he knows how to achieve it. His music constitutes a miracle of form; nothing lacks, and nothing is in excess. Neither redundancy nor dryness. Everywhere just the right note, and the precise affinity between what is said and what the artist wishes to say." André Suarès, La Revue musicale (December 1938).
ABOVE: *Photographic portrait of Maurice Ravel.*

installed, as well as central heating so as to fend off "humidity more penetrating than a Suarès thought." The composer even ventured to acquire a telephone, at the time still considered a daring plunge into modernity. Ravel, the son of an engineer, loved all the new technologies, gradually furnishing his house with an American refrigerator and the latest versions of radio and gramophone.

Manuel Rosenthal may have been a little severe in his opinion of Ravel's Belvédère. From the street, admittedly, the "slice of Camembert," with its fanciful Basque-style conical tower, makes a rather poor impression. The garden aspect, however, is another matter, for here reigns charm aplenty, what with the Japanese-style plantings and the timber-work balcony under a deep, overhanging roof.

Neither in his music nor in his comments was Ravel ever given to self-revelation. As Roland-Manuel remarked, a "singular sense of propriety always drove him to love clocks more than clockmakers and to feel more at one with trees than with human beings." Given

"Raised upon a rampart, a house with ground floor and upper storey forming a ground floor on the Rue Saint-Laurent, entrance to which is by steps on *the said street and a terrace on the east side. . . ." Bill of sale for the Belvédère (16 April 1921).* RIGHT: *Patterned wallpaper in the hallway.*

this, the Belvédère comes to seem almost as touching and sincere as an intimate journal. The beautiful furniture, like the fabrics and painted papers on the walls, bear witness to his taste, the countless bibelots to his curiosity and often his humor, and the exquisite details to his refinement.

Visitors exclaim over the handsome mahogany piano, its music rack set with an open score for the *Tombeau de Couperin*. They also take delight in the *japonaiseries* of the tiny parlor, asking where ever could the composer have found that pair of cups and saucers with the "artistically" pierced grounds. Equally amusing

ABOVE AND RIGHT: *R*avel himself took charge of the decoration, painting the backs of the Directoire chairs in the dining room and stenciling the ochre walls of his bedroom.

OPPOSITE: *Ravel transformed an old* cabinet de toilette *into his "small" library, which contains an abundance of handsomely bound books.*

is the little secret room, tucked away behind a vitrine in the "large" parlor and filled with books, papers, and various intriguing objects. So, too, the juxtaposition of the genuine and the fake, both on the walls and on the étagères. Nowhere is chance or error present without purpose, for it was through them that Ravel expressed an aesthetic truth. In response to Willy Goudeket, who

in 1933 asked the composer whether he liked surrounding himself with imitation works of art, Ravel replied: "There are lovable fakes. Furthermore, you will find [here] what you could very well take for old Chinese porcelain. Up close, you will discover that the designs represent something like the birth of Christ or

ABOVE: : *The "grand salon." During his travels and visits to antique shops, Ravel was always on the lookout for the refined, childish, or amusing bibelots he loved to collect at the Belvédère. His friends also contributed to the hoard.*

RIGHT: *The Japanese parlor. It was in this tiny room—Ravel himself was small—that the composer assembled the greatest concentration of his "lovable fakes."*

the Resurrection or yet the *Fêtes galantes* of Watteau. It was Madame du Barry to whom we owe these works of fantasy; she had them fabricated by the Compagnie des Indes. Moreover, those fakes were themselves imitated and therefore become delicate fake pastiches." Finally, Ravel asked: "Who in matters of art ever creates anything truly original?"

What most enchants visitors is the extraordinary collection of children's games, the puzzles, and the comical or poetic automatons, such as the nightin-

gale in a gilded cage flapping its wings and singing like those in the composer's *L'Enfant et les sortilèges.*

Anything Maurice Ravel ever said during an interview must be taken with a grain of salt. "I've replied to the journalists; I tell them nothing but jokes," he wrote in 1911. He was serious, however, when he stated in 1932: "At Montfort I spend every day at my

OPPOSITE: : *The music room with its beautiful mahogany piano. Over the instrument Ravel hung the portrait his mother painted by his Uncle Édouard. Open on the piano is the four-hand score for* Le Tombeau de Couperin.

workbench, and this is the only place where I can accomplish anything. Paris means nothing to me." Indeed, it was in the Belvédère that many of the composer's masterpieces came into being, among them *L'Enfant et les sortilèges* (completed in 1925), the Sonata for Violin and Piano (1923–1927), *Tzigane* (1922–1924), *Chansons madécasses* (1925–1926), *Boléro* (1928), the two Piano Concertos (1929–1931), etc.

In sum, Ravel's "solitude" at Montfort-l'Amaury is entirely relative. Mme Revelot, the governess who called the composer *Mon Maître,* continued her jealous watch over him. Every day he walked down into the village, bought the newspapers and his pack of Caporals, those potent Gauloises cigarettes to which he was addicted, and drank a Vermouth-Cassis on the terrace of the café in the town square. Then came the friends, pupils, and fellow composers, sometimes from afar, as in the case of Manuel de Falla and George Gershwin. Dinner at Ravel's table, always immaculately served, might consist of mackerel in white wine, very rare steak, and fruit from the orchard. There was also the occasional revel, such as the famous *"impromptu de Montfort-l'Amaury"* on 10 June 1928, when some thirty guests appeared, among them Joachim Nin, Arthur Honegger, Alexander Tansman, Pierre-Octave Ferroud, and Jane Bathori.

At regular intervals, however, Ravel would make his way back to Paris, indulging himself in an orgy of theatres, antique shops, concerts, and the jazz he adored. He could also be found at the famous "Boeuf sur le Toit," the roaring twenties cabaret frequented by Cocteau, Wiéner, and Doucet. He traveled throughout Europe as well as the United States, all the way to the Grand Canyon via New York and Boston. Always he returned to Montfort-l'Amaury, to the Belvédère the poet Léon-Paul Fargue called "that Jack-in-the-box toy, that house he partitioned and furnished like a cabin on a ship or a work basket, which he composed of precious and very particular objets, rather like those found in a tool kit or a toilet case."

As visitors return down the hill to the Place de l'Église, they may find themselves moved not only by the obsessive beat of *Boléro* but perhaps as well by a humble image, that of the bathroom in the Belvédère with its comb, toothbrush, and dressing gown.

Manuel de Falla
1876–1946

Incredible as it may seem, Manuel de Falla, the author of *El Amor Brujo* and *Nights in the Gardens of Spain*, never set foot in Granada before the spring of 1915, when he was already thirty-one.

Born on 23 November 1876 in Cadiz, Andalusia's port on the Atlantic, de Falla discovered at a very early age the two most essential dimensions of his character: his love of music and the Catholic faith. In 1896, having exhausted the musical possibilities available to him in Cadiz, young de Falla moved to Madrid in order to study piano at the Conservatory, where he would take all the highest honors. In the Spanish capital he also worked with Felipe Pedrell, the composer, musicologist, and folklorist who argued for an authentically Spanish music. "I owe him," de Falla confessed, "my initiation into an art ample, sincere, and based on popular song. I studied with him for six years, receiving his precious advice and perceiving, under his tender and wise protection, new and vast horizons."

In 1905, when the Fine Arts Academy staged a competition, de Falla won it with *La Vida breve*, a short two-act opera set in El Albaicin, Granada's gypsy quarter opposite the Alhambra. He knew the environment only from reading, but this was enough for Granada to become, in his imagination, a sort of chimerical horizon. Despite great effort and his competition prize, de Falla failed to have *La Vida breve* produced in Madrid. In 1907 he moved on to Paris, where he benefited enormously from his relationships with Claude Debussy, Maurice Ravel, Paul Dukas, Ricardo Viñes, and Isaac Albéniz. Finally, in 1913, *La Vida breve* was performed, to great acclaim, in both Paris and Nice. After war broke out in 1914 de Falla returned to Madrid, more Spanish than ever.

Now de Falla became friendly with a literary couple named María and Gregorio Martínez-Sierra,

"*M*anuel de Falla achieved mastery by a path which came ever closer to the Castilian mystics' 'Way of Perfection.'" Roland-Manuel, Manuel de Falla.

ABOVE: *Photographic portrait of "Don Manuel" (1910).*

whom he had met in Paris in 1913. Since 1911, however, he had known and studied their magnificent book entitled *Granada, Guia emocional*, its narrative illustrated by Gregorio Martínez-Sierra. Finally, in March and April 1915, the composer visited Granada with María Martínez-Sierra as his guide. The latter, in her autobiography, describes the "Aaah!" uttered by de Falla when he first laid eyes on the countryside around Granada, viewed from the Alhambra: "It was almost a cry. Simple admiration? The pleasure of having imagined from the pages of a book the charm he did not actually know? Pride at having known how to interpret it? The satisfaction of an artist who understood, with finesse, rhythm, and sound, how to reproduce the wonder of the thing unknown? No doubt it was all these things at once."

De Falla returned to Granada in the following year, this time as a colleague of Stravinsky and Diaghilev. *Nights in the Gardens of Spain (Noches en los jardines de España)*—a work also composed before he had ever seen Granada—was performed and warmly applauded. Meanwhile, the composer had under way the scores for *El corregidor* and *El sombrero de tres picos (The Three-cornered Hat)*, based on books by Gregorio and María Martínez-Sierra. He had also begun to dream of moving permanently in Granada, a step he actually took in 1919, following the death of his mother. At first he rented a house—now demolished—at Carmen de Santa Engracía 43. Then, in 1921, he moved to Calle Antequeruela Alta 11, together with his sister María del Carmen and his cat Confucio. Visitors, many of them famous, arrived in droves to see "Don Manuel," and a number of these have left descriptions of the place, among them José Mora Guarnido, the biographer of Federico García Lorca:

"In the Calle Antequeruela, situated on the side of the Alhambra hill which plunges into the River Genil, [de Falla] had a humble *carmencillo* ['small villa'], with a rose garden, honeysuckle, and jasmin, a grape arbor, pots of geraniums, and a fountain if my memory does not fail me. Best of all, however, was the location. The balconies overlooked the entire Genil Valley with the grand panorama of the Sierra Nevada in the background, and on the lower right the city extending towards the Vega plains and all punctuated with little

towers and treetops. The house was small but sufficient to the musician's minimal, even austere needs. On the ground floor, behind the large entrance door, was a flagstone-paved patio, the dining room, kitchen, and bathroom; on the upper storey, with a balcony—and what a balcony!—with a view over the *sierra*, his bedroom and that of María del Carmen. . . ."

The decoration—now recovered or reconstituted from photographs and period designs—is also of an almost monastic simplicity. Mathilde Pomès, who recounts a visit to Don Manuel at the beginning of the

"*F*rom my room
I hear the fountain

A tendril of vine,
a ray of sunshine.
They point to where my heart
is beating.

Through the August air,
clouds drifting.
I dream I do not dream
within the fountain.

Federico García Lorca,
"Granada and 1850."

1930s, was not in the least surprised by the musician's "maisonette": "I had already seen it. Yes, I must have seen it in paintings by [some Fra Angelico], in a seraphic garden, that sequence of white cells, with their polished and well-arranged furniture, their look of wisdom and purity, that whole atmosphere of care and attention in the backgrounds of a [fifteenth-century] *Annunciation*."

Don Manuel always received his callers with kindness and modesty. Tea was served—a fairly exotic drink in Spain—after which, inevitably, the musician began a ritual that never failed to impress visitors. Carefully taking a cigarette of blond tobacco from a box, he inserted it into one end of a small cardboard

"*It's a small intimate paradise fit for a sage; it's the house of a pure and sensitive being,*" wrote Émile Vuillermoz. In the same way, de Falla made "Los Espinillos," the little house where, after 1941, he lived in Argentine exile, a complete reflection of his unique personality.

chamber opera of 1923 based on an episode in *Don Quixote*, and the Concerto for Harpsichord, premiered by Wanda Landowska in 1926 in Madrid. These entrancing pieces reflected the composer's shift away from folkloric colorism towards a re-creation of the early polyphonic masters of Spain. De Falla also evinced a predilection for eighteenth-century French and Italian composers, but this in no way kept him from appreciating the music of his contemporaries, particularly that of his friends in the "Groupe des Six."

Soon after he settled in Granada, de Falla met a twenty-one-year-old poet who had yet to publish anything: Federico García Lorca. They immediately became close friends, indeed true soul mates. In 1922 the pair organized a *cante jondo* competition in Granada. In the following year, de Falla utilized the music for *Misterio de los Reyes magos (Mystery of the Three Kings)* —playing it himself on the piano—to accompany the little play with the same title, produced in Granada by Lorca for a marionette theatre. Together, de Falla and Lorca made the rounds of Andalusian villages collecting folksongs. "We made many excursions," wrote Isabel García Lorca, the poet's sister, because my father lent us his automobile every time Don Manuel wanted it. . . ."

Meanwhile, Manuel de Falla continued his activities in other cities—Madrid, Seville, and Barcelona but also Paris, Zurich, and London. Secure in his international fame, the tenant of the little house in the Calle Antequeruela would henceforth figure as well among the leading celebrities of Granada. In 1926, on the occasion of his fiftieth birthday, the municipality bestowed a title upon him: "Beloved child of the city." Sometimes, however, he grew weary of the fuss, the city's noise and bustle. And so, "once a year," he said, "I go to recuperate in solitude in a tiny Andalusian village, speaking to no one for ten or twelve days, so as to prepare myself for work."

Beginning in 1931, the political situation in Spain grew ominous, particularly in Andalusia. Meanwhile, de Falla dedicated himself more and more to a vast project entitled *Atlántida*, "a mystery both secular and religious, steeped in legends and marvels, its tone a balance of the epical, the mystical, and the popular," according to de Falla's biographer Jean-Charles Hoffelé.

tube, after which he used an ivory toothpick to push a tiny ball of cotton wool into the other end of the tube, where it would serve as a filter. The preparation over, de Falla lit the cigarette and smoked it, methodically "as if he were counting the puffs," according to one witness.

Next, de Falla led his guests upstairs, where he had installed his modest upright piano. A generous and gifted pianist, the composer loved playing and frequently invited his private audience to name the pieces they wanted to hear. Among the favorites were *El Retablo de Maese Pedro (Master Peter's Puppet Show)*, a

ABOVE: *The parlor on the ground floor where de Falla received his visitors in Granada, some of whom had traveled a great distance. Even now the* room *seems to resonate with the guitar and voice of Federico García Lorca.*
OPPOSITE: *The composer's simple upright piano.*

For this "scenic cantata" the composer made frequent sojourns in Majorca through June of 1934.

In July 1936 the Spanish Civil War broke out, whereupon Granada fell almost immediately into rebel hands. On 19 August the brilliant, multi-talented Federico García Lorca was murdered by the Falangists.

Thereafter Manuel de Falla secluded himself in his *carmencillo,* receiving only his closest friends or his neighbors and refusing all honors proposed by the new government. Finally, on 28 September 1939 he left Granada forever. A few days later he sailed on the *Neptunia* out of Barcelona and went into exile in Argentina. On 14 November 1946 de Falla died there in poverty, without ever having completed *Atlántida.*

*T*he bedroom of Manuel de Falla, where the furnishings and decoration say much about the composer's profound faith. Yet he composed only two short pieces of sacred music.

Francis

Poulenc

1899–1963

"Along a chalk slope," wrote Colette, "Poulenc lives surrounded by vineyards in a big, airy house, where he makes and drinks his own wine. Throughout his spangled orchestration, listen for the sound, watch for the shimmer of gold and the bubbles surging up from an opulent terrain! Look at Poulenc: are those the features of a water drinker? He's got a strong, sniffing nose, an eye quick to change expressions. He is confident and precautious, comfortable in friendship, and poet like a peasant."

In this charming portrait of Francis Poulenc at home in the Loire Valley, the great novelist conjured the right image even if she exaggerated a bit. Always quick to sense the subtle relationships between persons and places, Colette nonetheless went a bit far when she characterized Francis Poulenc as a wine grower, deeply rooted in the Tourain. The composer did indeed learn to cultivate the Vovray of his neighboring landowners, just as he conceived a deep love for the landscape and ever-changing skies of the Loire country, but never for a second did he forget or renounce his Parisian origins. It was in Paris that Poulenc was born on 7 January 1899, into a Parisian family, and it was in Paris that he spent his childhood and adolescence—provided one may annex the house of his grandparents in Nogent-sur-Marne.

Francis Poulenc, after studying piano with Ricardo Viñes ("I owe him everything") and composition with Charles Koechlin, became a celebrity at a very early age. The January 1920 issue of *Comœdia* carried two articles by the shrewd journalist and excellent composer Henri Collet, who announced that a young school of French musicians, the "Groupe des Six," had been born and that its godfathers were Jean Cocteau and Éric Satie. Actually, the six composers—Auric, Durey, Honegger, Milhaud, Poulenc, and Tailleferre—were more a band of friends than a stylistically coherent "school," though all of them drew inspiration from

"Parisian folklore," meaning street musicians, music halls, circus bands, etc. Still, the "Six" would share a common notoriety after the success and "scandal" of their collective theatre piece entitled *Les Mariés de la Tour Eiffel* (1921). As for Poulenc, his personal fame was assured following the triumph of the ballet *Les Biches* (1924), its score a witty amalgam of jazz-age sophistication and romantic lyricism.

At the age of sixteen Poulenc had lost his mother and then his father two years later, in 1917. The orphaned youth had the good luck to forge an affectionate relationship with an old friend of the family, Virginie Liénart, a great music lover whom Poulenc called "Aunt Liénart." This good woman allowed Francis the run of her apartment in Cannes and a small

Earthy and refined, iconoclastic and mystical, brilliant and tragic, rakish and lyrical, phonily naïve and ironically wise, Francis Poulenc was never merely what anyone thought he was. He remains, quite simply, one of the most vital French musicians of the twentieth century.

house, "La Lézardière," in Nazelles, not far from Amboise. Poulenc, who found it difficult to work in Paris as well as he would have liked, made extended stays in the Tourain. In 1927 he managed to acquire a large house in Noizay, four kilometers from Nazelles. It took a while to complete the transaction and move in, but on 3 December 1928 Poulenc could write to his friend Henri Sauguet: "What an autumn I've just spent! My life is more like that of a construction foreman than the life of a musician! Fortunately, the end of my struggles is in sight, and I'll have a big house that will always be open to you. . . ."

"Le Grand Coteau" is superbly situated on the side of a chalk hill, overlooking the vineyards, woods, and meadows that descend terrace by terrace all the way to the Loire. Poulenc, with perhaps a touch of atavism inherited from a great-great grandfather, took particular care of the gardens. When it came to the lower terrace he adopted a style of sober refinement, as explained in a letter of 1 October 1930 to Marie-Laure de Noailles: "Imagine a beautiful round fountain and at the center a column crowned by a capital and, spitting water, (guess what) three Henri III *mignons* with strawberries and little caps. . . . There will also be two Greeks with boxwood bushes with sand in two colors (Blessed Virgin blue and chrome yellow), two obelisks at the center of the Greeks, a sixteenth-century sundial, a stone table, and boxed yews."

Spread out in the clearing on the west side of the house is a maze of "troglodite" caves, excavated in the tuffa and used for making and storing wine. On the east side a promenade bordered by lime trees extends the upper terrace. The house—a sixteenth-century structure built during the reign of Henri II but then refurbished in the late eighteenth century—is quite simple, of medium size, and nicely proportioned. Neither a château nor a cottage, it is a place to live in, the "house of the sage," in the words of Princess Edmond de Polignac, to whom Poulenc dedicated his Concerto for Two Pianos as well as his Organ Concerto.

The ground floor comprises only three rooms: the studio (*cabinet de travail*), the dining room, and the large studio (*salon de travail*). Poulenc's extremely simple bedroom is upstairs. On this floor and the one above are the guest rooms, which during holidays were used

by members of his family, to whom the composer always remained very attached.

In the course of his frequent sojourns at Noizay, Poulenc undertook, continued, or completed a good many of his major works. An early riser given to composing "at the keyboard," he often woke his guests at

"[**F**rancis Poulenc] laid eggs like a cuckoo in all nests but his own, yet every nesting warbled pure Francis." Ned Rorem, An Absolute Gift (c. 1978).

OPPOSITE: The caves used for pressing grapes and making wine, seen through the trees along the promenade.
ABOVE: The terrace and the Loire Valley viewed from the composer's bedroom.

the crack of dawn. The two mahogany Pleyels in his studio, one a grand piano and the other an upright, remind us that the composer was also an exceptional pianist, one who created several works for two instruments, apart from the Concerto in B minor, the Sonata, the *Élégie*, and *L'Embarquement pour Cythère*. On the

ABOVE: *The studio of Francis Poulenc, observed from the very place where the composer worked, his back to the window so that birds in flight would not distract him from his task.*
RIGHT: *The medallion of the*

Black Virgin of Rocamadour above the keyboard of the Pleyel grand piano.
OPPOSITE: *Over the mantelpiece in the studio, the portraits of Ricardo Viñes, Claude Debussy, and Guillaume Apollinaire.*

grand piano's sounding board Poulenc had the medallion of the Black Virgin of Rocamadour affixed directly above the manufacturer's name. It was during his first visit to this mountain shrine, in August 1936, following the accidental death of his friend and fellow musician Pierre-Octave Ferroud, that Poulenc found himself "thinking of the frailty of our human existence." "Once again," he wrote, "I was drawn to the spiritual life. Rocamadour brought me back to the faith of my childhood." He immediately launched into the composition of his *Litanies to the Black Virgin*.

The studio, open and flooded with light, is also very functional. The two large bookcases attest to the composer's well-known taste for poetry, as well as his frequent study of scores by all the great masters, from Monteverdi to Schönberg. Poulenc, who loved radio and whose works were often recorded, furnished the studio with one of those big "receivers" which gave ample satisfaction to music lovers in the days before the decibel craze took possession of the auditory world. A fine portrait of Poulenc's mother hangs on the wall above the piano, supplemented on every side by casually arranged photographs of friends and a few cherished composers.

More than anything else, however, it is a trio of golden books on the piano that constitute the most eloquent testaments to the haven of friendship that Francis Poulenc's Noizay was. The promise made to Sauguet was richly fulfilled, and "Le Grand Coteau" became open house for a throng of musical, artistic, and literary personalities. Notes on their calling cards tell the story, as when the *foie gras* inspired Sauguet to scribble his praise in verse, or when Prokofiev felt moved to joke "do-sol-mi-do, my next symphony." Louise de Vilmorin penned a poem; Violette Treyfusis managed a compliment free of venom; and all manner of famous folk left signatures or comments: Colette, Picasso, the Polignacs, the Noailles, and, of course, the composer's interpreters. Among these were Pierre Bernac, who gave the first performances of so many songs; Yvonne Gouverné, to whom Poulenc dedicated several of his choral works; Jacques Février, his collaborator at the piano; and Georges Prêtre, the conductor who presided over the premiere of the opera *La Voix humaine*.

One dined well at Noizay, for Poulenc was a serious gourmand, and Anne, his irreplaceable cook, produced one triumphant terrine after another. One also

drank well, and the master of the house took infinite care with his wines. There was, to be sure, a lot of music-making, but not without abundant time to frolic with Poulenc's favorite dog, Mickey. Another pastime was bridge, particularly when Prokofiev, a passionate card player, stayed over. The Russian composer, however, had no liking for his host's music, which in no way offended Poulenc, who said: "Our relationship was a matter of bridge, the piano, and friendship." Poulenc, a man and an artist whom no one ever managed to capture in the banality of a definition, ventured this self-characterization: "The Noizay house, with its half-smiling, half-austere look, no doubt represents me fairly well."

Later in life, Francis Poulenc tended to follow the sun, to Cannes or to Bagnols-en-Forêt, when he was not traveling in Italy, the Netherlands, Switzerland, Portugal, and the United States. On 10 April 1963 he was scheduled to attend the premiere, at Carnegie Hall, of his Sonata for Clarinet and Piano, dedicated to the memory of Arthur Honegger. On 28 January, however, having just returned from a concert in Holland with the opera singer Denise Duval, he suddenly died in his Paris apartment at 5 Rue Médicis.

"You who, through the miracle of your genius, have the ability to sing better than anyone the grave poetry of a loaf of bread or a bowl of milk."
Francis Poulenc to Colette (22 August 1942).

TOP: In a group of portraits, that of Colette hangs at the center immediately above Raymond Radiguet.
ABOVE: Poulenc had a great interest in records, even those of his own compositions.

Bibliography

Joseph Haydn

Geiringer, Karl and I., *Haydn: A Creative Life in Music,* 3rd ed. Berkeley, 1982.

Landon, H.C.R., *Haydn: His Life and Music.* Bloomington, 1988.

Larsen, Jens P., *The New Grove Haydn* (1st American ed.). N.Y., 1983.

Marnat, Marcel, *Joseph Haydn, la mesure de son siècle.* Paris, 1995.

Vignal, Marc, *Joseph Haydn.* Paris, 1988.

Wolfgang Amadeus Mozart

Solomon, Maynard. *Mozart: A Life.* N.Y., 1995.

Landon, H.C. Robbins. *Mozart and Vienna.* London, 1991.

———, *Mozart: The Golden Years, 1781–1791.* London, 1989.

Massin, Jean and Brigitte, *Wolfgang Amadeus Mozart.* Paris, 1970.

Rech, Geza. *Visiting Mozart: A Guide to the Mozart Monuments in Salzburg.* Salzburg, c. 1969.

Ludwig van Beethoven

Autexier, Philippe A., *Beethoven: The Composer as Hero* (trans. by C. Lovelace). London, 1992.

Baker, Anne P., *Beethoven.* Phoenix Hill, 1997.

Cooper, Martin, *Beethoven, the Last Decade 1817–1827,* rev. Oxford and N.Y., 1985.

Johnson, Stephen, *Beethoven.* London, 1994.

Kerman, Joseph, and Alan Tyson, *The New Grove Beethoven.* N.Y., 1983.

Massin, Jean and Brigitte, *Ludwig van Beethoven.* Paris, 1967.

Matthews, Denis, *Beethoven.* London, 1985.

Schony, Heinz, *The Beethoven Memorial Sites Administered by the Vienna Municipal Museums.* Vienna, 1981.

Franz Schubert

Jackson, Stephen, *Franz Schubert: An Essential Guide to His Life and Works.* London, 1996.

Marek, George R., *Schubert.* N.Y., 1985.

Massin, Brigitte, *Franz Schubert.* Paris, 1993.

McKay, Elizabeth N., *Franz Schubert: A Biography.* Oxford and N.Y., 1996.

McLeish, Kenneth and Valerie, *Schubert.* London, 1979.

Reed, John, *Schubert,* 2nd ed. Oxford and N.Y., 1997.

Hector Berlioz

Barraud, Henry, *Hector Berlioz.* Paris, 1979.

Berlioz, Hector, *Mémoires.* Various editions.

Cairns, David, *Berlioz.* London, 1989.

Clarson-Leach, Robert, *Berlioz: His Life and Times.* Tunbridge Wells and N.Y., 1983.

Ole Bull

Haugen, Einar I., and Camilla Cai, *Ole Bull: Norway's Romantic Musician and Cosmopolitan Patriot.* Madison, 1993.

Smith, Mortimer, *The Life of Ole Bull.* Princeton, 1943.

Frédéric Chopin

Goncet, Odette, "Chopin à Nohant," *Le Piano-forte en France.* Paris, 1995.

Samson, Jim, *Chopin.* Oxford and N.Y., 1996.

Siepmann, Jeremy, *Chopin: The Reluctant Romantic.* London, 1995.

Zielinski, Tadeus A., *Frédéric Chopin.* Paris, 1995.

Franz Liszt

Demange, Odile, ed. and trans., *Franz Liszt, chronique biographique en images et en documents* (pref. by A. Brendel). Paris, n.d.

Huré, Pierre-Antoine, and Claude Knepper, eds., *Liszt en son temps.* Paris, 1987.

Taylor, Ronald Jack, *Franz Liszt: The Man and the Musician.* London, 1986.

Walker, Alan, *Franz Liszt.* London, 1971.

Watson, Derek, *Liszt.* London, 1989.

Williams, Adrian, *Portrait of Liszt: By Himself and His Contemporaries.* Oxford and N.Y., 1990.

Zaluski, Iwo and Pamela, *Young Liszt.* London and Chester Springs, 1997.

Richard Wagner

Anderson, Robert. *Wagner: A Biography.* London and Hamden, 1980.

Cotterill, Rowland, *Wagner.* Staplehurst, 1996.

Gray, Howard, *Wagner.* London and N.Y., 1990.

Gregor-Dellin, Martin, *Richard Wagner, His Life, His Work, His Century* (trans. by J.M. Brownjohn). San Diego, 1983.

La Famille Wagner et Bayreuth (album of photographs). Paris, 1976.

Millington, Barry, *Wagner.* London, 1984.

Ollivier, Blandine, ed., *L'Enchanteur et le roi des ombres: Choix de lettres de Richard Wagner et de Louis II de Bavière.* Paris, 1976.

Richard Wagner, sa vie à Lucerne. Lucerne, 1983.

Skelton, Geoffrey, *Richard and Cosima Wagner: Biography of a Marriage.* London, 1982.

Watson, Derek, *Richard Wagner: A Biography.* London, 1979.

Westbridge, John, *The New Grove Wagner.* N.Y., 1984.

Giuseppe Verdi

Hussey, Dyneley, *Verdi,* rev. London, 1973/1974.

Matz, Mary Jane Philipps, *Verdi* (French trans. by Gérard Gefen). Paris, 1996.

Mingardi, Corrado, *Con Verdi nella sua terra.* Busseto, 1994.

Osborne, Charles, *Verdi.* London, 1978.

Walker, Frank, *The Man Verdi* (intro. by P. Gossett). Chicago, 1982.

Wechsberg, Joseph, *Verdi.* London, 1974.

Johann Strauss II

Fantel, Hans, *Johann Strauss: Father and Son, and Their Era.* Newton Abbot, 1971.

Gartenberg, Egon, *Johann Strauss: The End of an Era.* University Park (PA), 1974.

Wechsberg, Joseph, *The Waltz Emperors: The Life and Times and Music of the Strauss Family.* N.Y., 1973.

Johannes Brahms

Frisch, Walter, *Brahms and His World,* 1990.

Holmes, Paul and Irene, *Brahms, His Life and Times.* Southborough, 1984.

MacDonald, Malcolm, *Brahms.* London, 1990.

Rostand, Claude, *Johannes Brahms.* Paris, 1978.

Swafford, Jan, *Johannes Brahms: A Biography.* N.Y., 1997.

Jules Massenet

Irvine, Demar, *Massenet: A Chronicle of His Life and Times.* Portland, 1994.

Massenet, Jules, *Mes Souvenirs* (ed. by G. Condé). Paris, 1992.

Edvard Grieg

Benestad, Finn, and Dag Schjelderup-Ebbe, *Edvard Grieg: The Man and the Artist* (trans. by W.H. Halverson and L.B. Sateren). Lincoln, 1988.

Horton, John, *Grieg.* London, 1974.

Vincent d'Indy

Gefen, Gérard, "César Franck, les franckistes et Chabrier," *Histoire de la musique occidentale.* Paris, 1985.

Thomson, Andrew, *Vincent d'Indy and His World.* Oxford and N.Y., 1996.

Vallas, Léon, *Vincent d'Indy* (Vol. I. *La Jeunesse* [1851–1886]; Vol. II. *La Maturité* [1886–1931]). Paris, 1946–1950.

Edward Elgar

Anderson, Robert, *Elgar.* London, 1993.

Kennedy, Michael, *Portrait of Elgar,* 3rd ed. Oxford and N.Y., 1987.

Moore, Jerrold Northrop, *Edward Elgar: A Creative Life.* Oxford and N.Y., 1984.

———, *Elgar: A Life in Photographs.* Oxford, 1972.

———, *Spirit of England: Edward Elgar in His World.* London, 1984.

Giacomo Puccini

Carner, Mosco, *Puccini: A Critical Biography,* 3rd ed. London, 1992.

Marggraf, Wolfgang, *Giacomo Puccini* (trans. by K. Michaelis). N.Y., 1984.

Southwell-Sander, Peter, *Puccini.* N.Y., 1996.

Addresses of Composers' Houses

Wilson, Conrad, *Giacomo Puccini.*
London, 1997.

Carl Nielsen
Caron, Jean-Luc, *Carl Nielsen.*
Lausanne, 1990.
Lawson, Jack, *Carl Nielsen.* London,
1997.
Nielson, Carl, *La Musique et la vie*
(French trans. by E. Berg-
Gravenstein and A. Artaud).
Paris, 1988.
———, *My Childhood.* Copen-
hagen, n.d.

Jean Sibelius
Layton, Robert, *The World of
Sibelius.* London, 1970.
Richards, Guy, *Jean Sibelius.*
London, 1997.
Tawaststjerna, Erik, *Sibelius* (trans.
by R. Layton). Berkeley, 1976.

Franz Lehár
Grun, Bernard, *Gold and Silver:
The Life and Times of Franz Lehár.*
London, 1970.

Maurice Ravel
Fondation Maurice Ravel, *Cahiers
Maurice Ravel.* Paris, n.d.
Larner, Gerald, *Maurice Ravel.*
London, 1996.
Marnat, Marcel, *Maurice Ravel.*
Paris, n.d.
———, ed., *Ravel* (as recalled by
Manuel Rosenthal). Paris.
Milon, Yves, *Maurice Ravel à
Montfort-l'Amaury* (photos by
Thomas Renaut). Paris.

Manuel de Falla
Crichton, Ronald. *Falla.* London,
1982.
Hoffelé, Jean-Charles, *Manuel de
Falla.* Paris, 1992.
"Manuel de Falla, musicien," *Poesia*
(French ed.), nos. 36-37. 1993.

Francis Poulenc
Chimènes, Myriam, ed.,
Correspondance: 1910–1963. Paris,
1994.
Hell, Henri, *Francis Poulenc,* rev.
Paris, 1978.
Ivry, Benjamin, *Francis Poulenc.*
London, 1996.

Haydn
Haydn Museum, Haydngasse 19
Vienna, Austria

Mozart
Gedenkstätte "Figarohaus"
Domgasse 5, Vienna, Austria

Beethoven
Gedenkstätte "Pasqualatihaus"
Mölker Bastei 8, Vienna, Austria

Gedenkstätte "Heiligenstädter
Testament," Probusgasse 6
Vienna, Austria

Schubert
Geburtshaus, Nussdorferstrasse 54
Vienna, Austria

Sterbwohnnung,
Kettenbrüchkengasse 6
Vienna, Austria

Berlioz
Maison et Musée Hector Berlioz
69, rue de la République
La Côte-Saint-André, France

Bull
Museet Lysøen
5215 Lysekloster
Bergen, Norway

Chopin
Château de George Sand
Nohant (Berry), France

Liszt
Liszt Haus, Marienstrasse 17
Weimar, Germany

Wagner
Haus Wahnfried
Richard Wagner Museum
Richard Wagner Strasse 48
Bayreuth, Germany

Verdi
Pialenza 21, Sant' Agata
Villanova sull' Arda, Italy
(open by appointment)

Strauss II
Praterstrasse 54
Vienna, Austria

Brahms
Maximilianstrasse 85
Baden-Baden, Germany

Massenet
Château d'Égreville
Égreville, France
(open by apppointment)

Grieg
Troldhaugen
Olav Kyrres Gate II
Bergen, Norway

d'Indy
Château des Faugs, Boffres
Alboussière, France
(open by appointment)

Elgar
The Elgar Foundation
Elgar's Birthplace
Crown East Lane
Lower Broadheath, Worcester
Great Britain

Puccini
Villa Puccini, Torre del Lago
Tuscany, Italy

Nielsen
Carl Nielsen Museet &
Barndomshjem
Claus Bergs Gade II
Odense, Denmark

Sibelius
Ainola Foundation
Alipostinkuja 6
Tuusula, Finland

Lehár
Villa Franz Lehár
Lehárkai 8
Bad Ischl, Austria

Ravel
5, rue Maurice Ravel
Montfort-l'Amaury, France

De Falla
Paseo de los Martires, Alhambra
Granada, Spain

Poulenc
Private estate in the Loire Valley

The photographers express their gratitude to the following:

Michel Stockhem, musicologist; Sigrid Pichler of the Wiener Yourismusverband; the directors of the
Historisches Museum der Stadt Wien; Helmut Haas, Mayor of Bad Ischl; Jean Boyer, President of the Association
Hector Berlioz; M. Lecard, President of the Fondation Maurice Ravel; and Dr. Wolfgang Amanshauser.
Also the composers' families and the curators of the various houses and collections: Maria Sams, Mme Boucard,
Berit Høgheim, Angela Jahn, Mme Hecker, Erling Dahl, Taru Ojajarvi, Mme Moreau, Mme Bessand-Massenet, Mme Iaria,
Françoise Melebeck, Eva Walquist, Melanie Weatherley, Hanna Birger Christensen; M. and Mme Jacques d'Indy,
M. and Mme Seringe, M. and Mme Carlo and Marianne Frediani, Alberto Carrara-Verdi, Sven Friedrich, Aldo Giarizzo,
A. Navarro Linares, Karsten Eshilsem, M. Cioffi, and M. Franco.

Photographic credits for the composers' portraits

Haydn: Gesellschaft der Musikfreunde, Vienna
Mozart: Mozart Museum, Salzburg
Beethoven: rights reserved
Schubert: Historisches Museum der Stadt Wien, Vienna
Berlioz: Conservatoire National Supérieur de Musique, Paris
Bull: Museet Lysøen, Bergen
Chopin: rights reserved
Liszt: Collection Ernest Burger, Munich
Wagner: Museum Richard Wagner, Lucerne
Verdi: rights reserved
Strauss II: Historisches Museum der Stadt Wien, Vienna
Brahms: Bibliothèque Musicale Gustave Mahler, Paris
Massenet: Collection Sirot, Paris
Grieg: Nina and Edvard Grieg's Home, Bergen
D'Indy: rights reserved
Elgar: private collection
Puccini: Museo della Scala, Milan
Nielsen: Danish Embassy, Paris
Sibelius: Ainola Foundation, Tuusula
Lehár: Lehár Museum, Bad Ischl
Ravel: Bibliothèque Nationale, Paris
De Falla: Bibliothèque Nationale, Paris
Poulenc: Collection Lipnitzki-Viollet, Paris

Translated by DANIEL WHEELER

Editor in chief: JEAN-JACQUES BRISEBARRE
Associate editor: IRÈNE NOUAILHAC
Editor: COLETTE VÉRON
Layout: RONAN GUENNOU
Design and production: Archipel Concept, Paris—Grignan

First published in the United Kingdom in 1998 by Cassell

This paperback edition published in 2000 by
Seven Dials, Cassell & Co.
Wellington House, 125 Strand
London, WC2R 0BB

Volume copyright © Éditions du Chêne - Hachette Livre, 1997
English translation © The Vendome Press, 1998

All rights reserved. No part of this publication may be reproduced in any material form (including photocopying
or storing it in any medium by electronic means and whether or not transiently or incidentally to some other use
of this publication) without the written permission of the copyright owner, except in accordance with the provisions
of the Copyright, Designs and Patents Act 1988 or under the terms of a licence issued by the Copyright Licensing
Agency, 90 Tottenham Court Road, London W1P 9HE. Applications for the copyright owner's written permission
to reproduce any part of this publication should be addressed to the publisher.

A CIP catalogue record for this book is available
from the British Library

ISBN 1-84188-063-9

Printed and bound in Spain